Common Ground

Common Ground

Writings on Family, Change, Loss & Resilience

Lynn Haraldson

Deeds Publishing | Athens

Copyright © 2021—Lynn Haraldson

ALL RIGHTS RESERVED—No part of this book may be reproduced in any form or by any electronic or mechanical means, including information storage and retrieval systems, without permission in writing from the authors, except by a reviewer who may quote brief passages in a review.

Published by Deeds Publishing in Athens, GA
www.deedspublishing.com

Printed in The United States of America

Cover design by Mark Babcock.

ISBN 978-1-950794-35-5

Books are available in quantity for promotional or premium use. For information, email info@deedspublishing.com.

First Edition, 2021

10 9 8 7 6 5 4 3 2 1

For my children: Carlene, Cassandre, Andrew, and Kevin, whose trust and permission to write about their lives made me a better writer.

Contents

Acknowledgments	ix
Introduction	xi
1. Minnesota	1
Growing up in Lake Wobegon	2
Camping Adventures in the Bear Coffin	5
The Burning Bed	6
'Twas the Night Before the Night Before Christmas	8
Bruce	10
A Mother's Day Story	13
The Pause	16
Anger: His	17
Anger: Mine	21
Running Naked Through a Graveyard	26
Lutefisk	29
Summer Vacation	30
Marty	34
Epilogue	39
2. Grief	41
The Song Remains The Same	41
The Forgiveness Train	44
A Time to Weep	46
Grief 101	49

Courtney Love	54
About Last Night	57
Grief Really Shouldn't End	58
Firsts	60
A Love that Could Never Be	63

3. Parenting — 67

Sixteen-Year-Old Life Changer	68
Staying One Step Ahead of the Second Child	70
Little Women Meet Ren and Stimpy	73
Thoughts on a Belly-Button Piercing	75
Blackbird Fly	78
Signing Papers	81
Signing Papers II	83
Twin Daughters of Different Fathers	86
Christmas Invasion	89
Date Night	91
Shopping and the (Reluctant) Teenage Boy	93
Music, Movies, and the (Reluctant) Stepmother	95
The Yin & Yang of Stepparenting	97
Twelve Hours Later…	98
A Not-So-Martha-Stewart Thanksgiving	99
I Need to Be Needed	101
The Boys Are Back in Town	103
Mother's Day Music	104
Blackbird Revisited	110
In the Fight of His Life	112
Epilogue	114

4. On Being a Grandparent — 117

See You in October!	118
Buoyant	120
Today's the Day!	122
It's A…Claire!	123
I Finally Feel like a Grandma. Or is it Grammy?	124

Once a Mother, Always a Mother	126
Grammy Nanny	127
Auntie Carly	132
It's Your Second Birthday…Already?	133
The Walk	136
They'll All Fit	139
Audrey Rose	140

5. Weight Part 1 — The Greatest Hits — 143

One Thing	144
Who's That Girl?	146
Oprah (2007)	147
People, Today, & *Entertainment Tonight*	156
CNN	164
No More Apologies	168

6. Biking — 171

Bike Envy	172
I Know I Can	173
Fast Star	175
Zen and the Art of Bicycle Maintenance	177
The Best Worst Bike Ride Ever	180
Clearing My Head	183
Seven Times Slower	185
It's Like Riding a Bike	186

7. Weight Part 2 — The B Sides — 191

I Still Believe	192
"I did dit!"	194
Flawed and…Inspiring?	196
Throwing Out The Three-Hundred-Pound Pitch	198
Pulling Back the Sheets: Intimacy and Body Image	200
Vulnerable	202
Adventures in Maintenance: Letters to Santa*	205
Lessons Learned from a Three-Legged Cat	207

Own It!	210
Boom. Done.	212
Weight-Loss Dropout	214
What's Real, What's True, What's On Repeat?	217
The Fine Line Between Compliment and Judgement	220
8. The Post-Divorce Years	**223**
Hot Water's On the Right	224
Life Lessons in a Laundromat	225
Learning the Ropes	227
Let the Mauling Begin	229
Like Buttons in a Biscuit Tin	232
The Polar Vortex	235
Ready!	237
The Department of Happiness Has Reopened	238
Letting Go	240
When Love Comes to Town	242
Care in the Time of Covid-19	244
Epilogue	246
About the Author	**247**

Acknowledgments

My friend and political verbal sparring partner, Rodney Sherman, was the catalyst that brought me to writing as a career. It's amazing how a simple phone call can change your life. From that phone call I met Paul Hambke, my first editor. Without him, I would have no body of work to publish. Thank you for your encouragement and tough love. You knew I had it in me even when I didn't think so.

Thank you to my writing professors, Cass Dalglish, Barbara Anderson, and John Schmit at Augsburg University in Minneapolis, and Ron Shumaker at Clarion University of Pennsylvania. Thanks also to fellow blogger Shauna Reid, whose friendship and mentoring both in writing and in life continues to push me closer to believing in myself, and friend and copyeditor Gail Gedan Spencer, whose encouragement came at all the right times and who kept me consistent.

Thank you to my children, sisters Debbie and Emily, and brother-in-law Steve for your constant encouragement and for putting up with my questions and all the reading I've asked you to do. Knowing I can talk things out with all of you keeps my head in the game instead of the refrigerator.

Most of all, I thank my readers who, over the years, have offered their feedback, engaged in conversations with me and other readers, and stayed with me through the creatively dry years. You are the reason I write.

Introduction

When I was a kid, I really wanted to be a firefighter and paramedic like the guys on the TV show *Emergency!* But when I took a career assessment test in ninth grade, the results showed that my ideal career was barge loader.

Forty-five years later, that still makes me laugh.

I assure you that barge loader was not the career path I followed. In fact, I had no career in mind until I was thirty-three and a friend, who was a reporter for our local newspaper, called and asked me if I'd be interested in writing for them "once in a while." Once in a while turned into a full-time job, starting at $12,000 a year. Not great pay, but the health insurance was good and I was a single mother of two.

I was in charge of good news, writing features about interesting local people and taking photos of one-year-olds for the First Birthdays section. I was also the engagements, weddings, and sports copyeditor. Using grid paper, I laid out the Lifestyles, School, and Church pages on deadline days, and I rolled black and white film and developed photos in the dark room. It was the best job I ever had.

Each Thursday, the paper ran an editorial section. It featured an editorial, letters to the editor, and an op-ed column written by one of the two news writers or the editor. Columnists, to me, were rock stars.

On my bookshelves were collections of columns by Ellen Goodman, Molly Ivins, and Anna Quindlen, and I regularly read Leonard Pitts, Jr., Mark Murray, Dave Barry, Jeanne Marie Laskas, and George Will. I admired the fluidity of column writing and how columnists could tell a story or argue a point in fifteen-hundred words or less.

Ten months after I was hired, the editor wanted me to start my own op-ed column. I objected, arguing that I had nothing to write about. But his wasn't a request, and on July 10, 1997, my column, "Been There, Done That" debuted on page four. My first topic was about weddings and how I was never a bridesmaid, always a bride. It drew a few laughs and some eyerolls, but my column writing got better as I gained confidence in exploring personal, local, and global issues and sharing them in print.

Letters and comments from readers were (usually) my favorite part about writing a column. Topics such as grief and family always drew the most positive and heartfelt responses. Columns about (my) politics or anything pertaining to (my interpretation of) the Bible were usually met with not such favorable criticism. Either way, I was in a conversation with readers, and for me, that was the whole point of writing a column.

Blogging was fairly new when I began a diet in 2005. My goal was lofty: I wanted to lose at least one hundred fifty pounds. To help me with the process, I created a blog in which I shared my frustrations, milestones, and goals with people who were also working through weight issues. Readers and other bloggers were my support network, and me theirs. Around the same time, I launched a creative nonfiction blog, Zen Bag Lady, which was more in the vein of "Been There, Done That," something that, by then, I was writing intermittently as a freelancer.

When I began selecting columns and blogs to include in this collection, I focused on finding the best ones, Lynn's Greatest Hits. Then a chance encounter with Bruce Springsteen, or at least his voice on NPR's *Fresh Air*, put me on to a different focus. Terry Gross asked him if he felt the songs he'd written years ago have a different meaning now. He answered, "The wonderful thing about my job is you can revisit your twenty-two-year-old self or your twenty-four-year-old self any particular night you want. The songs pick up some extra resonance, I hope…And the songs themselves do broaden out as time passes and take on subtly different meanings, take on more meaning, I find."

I went back and looked at my writing through a wider lens, one with broadened meaning and resonance. I was able to see how each piece is a personal statement or a search for clarity.

It was like how Anna Quindlen explained what it was like writing her column, Public and Private, for the *New York Times*: "Never did I make so much sense of my life as I did then, for it was inevitable that as a writer I would find out most clearly what I thought, and what I only thought I thought, when I saw it written down."

Collectively, I saw how my words shaped my experiences and belief systems. This revamped vetting process allowed me to consider pieces that are more like B sides than greatest hits, but have picked up extra resonance when considered within the whole chapter.

Unlike a personal journal, which can offer the same insight over the years, these published works allowed me to engage in conversations with readers searching for the same clarity and understanding in their own lives. I hope you find yourself in some of my stories. Maybe somewhere you'll nod your head and say, "Been there, done that."

1. Minnesota

I was born in Minneapolis on August 14, 1963, exactly ten years after my brother, Marty. I always tell him I was the best birthday gift he got that day. He says it was the transistor radio. He's mistaken. It was me.

Several famous people share my birth year: Johnny Depp, Tori Amos, John Stamos, Mike Meyers, Brad Pitt, Coolio, Quentin Tarantino, Larry the Cable Guy, and Charles Barkley. We were born at the apex of the Baby Boom and Gen X, in the age of Madison Avenue, "Duck and Cover," and the space race. Martin Luther King gave his "I Have a Dream" speech two weeks after I was born, and JFK was assassinated in November.

In Minnesota in 1963, the tallest building was still the Foshay Tower in downtown Minneapolis; Harmon Killebrew and the Twins, and Fran Tarkenton and the Vikings played ball at Metropolitan Stadium; the Guthrie Theater opened; and Hubert Humphrey was a senator.

My family at that time included Dad, Mom, Marty, sister Debbie, and me, and we lived in the then-bourgeoning suburb of Bloomington. In 1966, my brother Matthew was born.

In 1972, we moved to Jasper, a small town in the southwest corner of the state where my parents grew up. Marty, who was in college, remained in Bloomington.

In 1975, my mom, age forty three, and dad, forty four, were surprised by another pregnancy, and my sister Emily was born.

Two years later, Dad was offered his former job in the Twin Cities, and we moved again. I graduated from high school in 1981 and, missing what I considered my hometown, I moved back to the Jasper area, where I got married and had a baby, in that order. But my husband died eleven days after our daughter was born. In a haze of grief, I got pregnant a year later with my second daughter. I was married and divorced and married again before moving to Pennsylvania in 1991.

This exhaustive timeline reflects the complicated relationship I have with Minnesota and its memories, both the incredible highs and the desperate lows. But as Garth Brooks sings, "I could have missed the pain, but I'd have had to miss the dance." It's why, no matter where I live, if someone asks me where I'm from, I will always say, "I'm from Minnesota."

Growing up in Lake Wobegon
Posted January 2002

I had no expectation that the live broadcast of *A Prairie Home Companion* would come in clearly, if at all, on the clock radio in our cabin in the middle of Cook Forest. Static-free public radio is a rarity in rural Pennsylvania, but being a die-hard PHC fan, I had to try. The moon, the stars, the trees, and the hills must have aligned because I was not only able to find a public radio station, but Garrison Keillor's voice was as clear as if I was sitting in the front row of the Fitzgerald Theater.

Keillor's fictional town of Lake Wobegon, Minnesota, "Where all the women are strong, all the men are good-looking, and all the children are above average," could be anywhere. If you change the residents' names from Johansson to Ochs, Ingvist to Schmader, and Lindstrom to Buzzard, Lake Wobegon could be towns in western Pennsylvania like New Bethlehem, Sligo, or Knox. Instead of the Side Track Tap, there's the Dew Drop Inn near Lucinda. Marble doesn't have a Chatterbox Cafe, but it has Montana's Restaurant. Shippenville's version of Ralph's Pretty Good Grocery is the Red and White.

My Lake Wobegon was Jasper, Minnesota. Like the fictional town, there was a grocery store (that my family owned), a café, a bowling alley, one bar, and two hardware stores. There were also several churches, and my family belonged to the American Lutheran Church, which was known to the old timers as the Norwegian Church.

The ALC was built of Jasper quartzite, a hard pink and gray colored stone quarried in the town's backyard. My aunt Mavis was the organist and her husband Vic was head usher. Every Sunday we sat on the right side, sixth row up from the front, always entering the pew in the same order with my little brother and I separated by Mom.

We were *not* allowed to turn around. Ever.

When we were little, Mom packed Cheerios, marshmallows, and chocolate chips, and when we were older, Dad supplied us with Lifesavers or Certs. If he forgot, or if he only had wintergreen (not my favorite), he always had Rolaids.

If there were flowers on a stand near the altar, that meant there had been a funeral during the week, which meant there might be leftover food in the church kitchen. Children's choir practice was every Wednesday after school, and my friends and I would raid the kitchen for ham sandwiches or coleslaw. Typically all that was left, though, were jars of sweet pickles and mayonnaise.

I'd be awash in these deep thoughts about funeral food and sucking on my fourth Lifesaver when Dad nudged me with the offering plate, and I would put in my envelope with a quarter from my piggy bank.

When the service was over and the pastor and the adult choir had filed out of the church during the last hymn, we all remained seated until Vic dismissed us row by row. Mavis played the organ until everyone shook hands with the pastor, which could take a while depending how chatty people were that day or if they brought visitors. We'd slowly walk up the aisle, but it gave me time to see all the people I wasn't allowed to turn around and see earlier. I'd give a little wave to both of my grandmothers, and mouth "hi" to my friends, who I would see later in Sunday school, unless they got lucky and were going home after church.

Every year, the Sunday evening before Christmas, the first-through sixth-grade Sunday school classes put on a Christmas pageant. We practiced for six weeks preparing for our big night. I was always a narrator because I was a good reader, which I didn't mind until sixth grade when I wanted more than anything to play Mary. It was my last chance to put on the blue robe, look holy, and gaze at the plastic Jesus in the manger. But as usual, I was the narrator. I complained to my parents and they said it was more important to tell the story than to play Mary. Shows how much they knew.

The sanctuary had a thirty-foot peaked ceiling and ten-foot gothic style arched stained glass windows on the outside walls. The choir loft was perpendicular to the altar where, on that one night, kids were allowed to sit. On Sunday mornings, the church was lit primarily with daylight. On our Christmas program night, the candles and ceiling chandeliers sparkled and glowed in a way that could make even the staunchest skeptic believe a child was born in a barn, and angels sang to a bunch of shepherds two thousand years ago.

After the performance, we each got a bag filled with peanuts, ribbon candy, and an orange, and we'd exchange gifts with our Sunday school teachers. It was the only night we are allowed to talk and laugh (and turn around) in the sanctuary.

The church looks the same today as it did thirty years ago. I was married there, my husband's funeral was held there, our daughter was baptized there, and within two years of each other, I said goodbye to my grandmothers there. Even though I live a thousand miles away from that beautiful Norwegian church, it is still a part of me, just like the grocery store, the café, the bowling alley, and all the other places and people now long gone in that small town on the prairie.

Camping Adventures in the Bear Coffin
Posted June 2007

Dad bought a homemade pop-up camper in 1969 that my mother dubbed the Bear Coffin. It was built on a 1953 Buick suspension, and when collapsed, it didn't lay flat like commercial pop-ups. Rather, it was shaped like an igloo due to the bowed wood sides that folded out into beds. And as if it didn't look odd enough, Dad painted it the same vintage gold as our dining room. It caused a lot of rubbernecking as we drove down the highway, and it was always the talk of any campground we set up in.

In the front was a "kitchen" with a one-burner stove and tiny sink, and a small chemical toilet that let us avoid middle-of-the-night runs to the campground bathroom. Four people could sleep comfortably, but there were usually more than four of us on vacation, which meant that one or more of us either took a chance sleeping on the floor in between the beds, or slept in the station wagon.

Dad told us the Bear Coffin was sensitive to rain, and that there was a chance it could leak during a storm, particularly if someone touched the canvas. I was an overly imaginative child and given to hyperbole to explain things I didn't understand. I had no idea what a canvas was, and I didn't hear the "v" in the word when he was explaining, so what I heard Dad say was, "Don't ever, under any circumstance, touch the Kansas when it's raining, because a flood as big as Noah's will come and sweep you away, and you'll never see your family again." My little brother knew my fears, and every time it rained, he made sure I was watching when he held his finger a breath away from the canvas, making me scream, "Don't touch the Kansas!" Being the sensitive people they are, my family has not let me forget.

Despite its potential for catastrophic harm, the canvas had a wonderful outdoorsy smell that went well with the smell of my ancient dark green cloth sleeping bag with layers of stuffing. I would go to sleep listening to Mom and Dad visiting outside with other campers, waking only briefly when they would come in for the night and Dad shut the door, which sounded like the hatch of a space ship.

The Burning Bed
Posted February 2002

For a moment one evening last week, it was 1978. The dishes were done and the leftovers put away. The children were downstairs, my husband was upstairs. The living room was all mine. I lit candles and sunk into my favorite chair. An hour passed, then my daughter walked in and yelled, "Oh my god, Mom! The bookcase is on fire!" and right then I was fourteen and my twelve-year-old brother was in my bedroom yelling, "Wake up, Lynn! My bed is on fire!"

"What?" I whispered, half-asleep. "You're sleep walking. Go back to bed." But he kept shaking me and yelling at me to wake up.

"Where's Steve?" I asked, smelling smoke. Our parents and older sister were out of town to attend a funeral, so my brother-in-law was staying with us.

"He's not here!" Matthew yelled over his shoulder as he ran back into the hall. I followed him and sure enough, flames were shooting up his bedroom walls. He filled a bucket of water from the bathtub and I got a blanket thinking I could smother the flames, but there was no way we could put it out. We shut the door and Matthew went to wake up our three-year-old sister while I went downstairs to call the fire department. A woman answered, that much I remember, but the rest of our conversation is vague. My voice was shaking and my mouth was dry. I think I babbled something about "please hurry."

Standing on the driveway, we heard a siren in the distance. From the outside, it didn't look like our house was on fire. It was quiet and the stars were out. Although it was May, we could see our breath and Emily was shaking. Matthew found an old blanket in the garage and I wrapped her up. We'd recently moved to the neighborhood and I didn't know the neighbors very well, but we couldn't stay outside. With Emily in my arms, I went next door and rang the doorbell while Matthew stayed to wait for the fire trucks. A minute later, the neighbor's door opened, and after a brief explanation, she invited us in. Emily and I sat on the couch with a view of our house from the glass front door.

Steven arrived just ahead of the police. He was surprised to find Matthew outside and apologized profusely when he learned of the fire. He'd only been gone for fifteen minutes to retrieve some medication from his apartment a few blocks away and was stunned by what had transpired in such a short time.

The fire trucks turned on to our street without sirens, but the flashing lights looked like a carnival ride. Firefighters in yellow jackets ran into our house with hoses, yelling, and soon glass was breaking. A flaming mattress toppled out of Matthew's second-floor window into the backyard. More glass was broken and smoke poured out from my bedroom window.

When the fire was out, the fire captain, a tall gentle-looking man came to talk to me and to make sure my sister and I hadn't suffered smoke inhalation. I assured him I was fine. Emily just stared at him. The fire, he said, started when a nightlight overheated and caught a blanket on fire. We were all lucky Matthew woke up, he added.

The captain said they'd be there a while, so Steve took us to his apartment to sleep. At dawn, I walked back to the house to see the damage and to check on my parakeet. I didn't think he'd survive the smoke, and if he did, the house was cold since so many windows were broken. I wasn't yet in the driveway when I smelled the burnt remains. The smell of smoke from a house fire isn't like the smell of burning logs in a fireplace. Once it's in your nose, you never forget it. When I walked in the house, my parakeet started singing (or maybe scolding me) from his cage in the living room. He was fine, but the upstairs was not. The walls in the stairway were streaked with black and the stairs were wet and muddy from the firefighter's boots and hoses.

Everything upstairs—the bathroom counter, toilet, tub, dressers, carpets, beds, nightstands, lamps, homework, books, stereos—was coated in a smooth gray soot. In my closet, my pink confirmation dress and white shoes were tinted black. My brother's room was burned beyond the wall studs. His bed frame, curtains, dresser, posters, and closet were all were crisp, curled, charred, and singed.

Now, twenty four years later, a candle in my living room was completely melted on one side and its flame had lit a wooden picture frame on fire. It frightened me the same as when I was fourteen, and while I was able to contain it quickly, I wondered what would have happened if my daughter hadn't come in at just that moment.

I received a letter the other day asking for a donation for our local fire company. I hope I never need them, but I'm glad I'm alive to mail them a check.

'Twas the Night Before the Night Before Christmas
Posted December 2007

Every Christmas, we opened gifts on Christmas Eve, which meant that Santa came to our house the night before the night before Christmas. Our parents convinced us that Santa started his trip at our house before heading to the International Date Line, where it was already the next day. It made total sense to me, until I cracked the whole Santa thing when I was ten. More on that in a minute.

Each Christmas Eve, Dad would read the Christmas story from the Bible. I always felt sad for Baby Jesus. What was a kid supposed to do with gold, frankincense, and myrrh? Sure, I got boring things like socks and underwear for Christmas, but there were usually a few things from my Sears catalog wish list, too.

One gift in particular remains the most mysterious I've ever received. I was a senior in high school. The week before Christmas in 1980, I came home after working the dinner shift at Country Kitchen and found a large tin can on the front stoop. On top was written, "To Lynn From Santa." I brought it inside and asked if anyone knew who left it. My dad said it wasn't there when he came home from work, and no one had heard a car pull up in the drive.

The can was about twelve inches tall and decorated with a holiday scene. Whatever was inside had been sealed like a can of peas and could only be opened with a can opener. I brought it to the kitchen and dug around in the utensil drawer. My mother called out from the family room, "You can't open that until Christmas!"

"But why?" I asked. "We don't even know who it's from!"

That didn't matter. Haraldson Christmas Rule Number One: No gift shall be opened until Christmas Eve. No exceptions. So I spent a few hours analyzing the handwriting on the lid, the same way I did when I cracked the mystery of Santa.

Santa always left a note of thanks for the cookies and milk, and when I got old enough to notice, I realized he used the notepaper my mom kept in the cupboard. It disturbed me to think of some old guy wandering around our house looking for paper and a pen. It was bad enough that we didn't have a fireplace and had to leave the front door unlocked so Santa could get in, but imagining him turning on lights and sifting through the cupboard made me a little uncomfortable.

I was relieved the year I realized Santa had the same handwriting as my dad, only I had to keep it under wraps because my little brother was too young to figure it out. I felt superior with this knowledge and was quite smug the following year when he learned who Santa was.

"I've known for a long time," I told him.

"Well la-di-da," he replied, and stuck his tongue out at me.

This time, the handwriting wasn't so obvious. Was it a boy's writing? A girl's? I couldn't tell. There were a few strange regulars at the restaurant who might leave me gifts outside my house, but that was too creepy to think about for very long. I wasn't dating anyone seriously, and definitely not anyone of mystery or intrigue. Out of guesses, there was nothing more I could do but let the can sit under the tree for seven torturous days.

On Christmas Eve, I sat on the couch with a can opener in my hand. Dad read the Christmas story. Then my little sister opened her first gift. Then my little brother opened his first gift. (Haraldson Christmas Rule Number Two: Gifts are opened in order, according to age.) When it was finally my turn, I cranked open the can as fast as I could. Inside was a teddy bear and a note: "Merry Christmas. Love, Dad."

Bruce
Posted March 2007

I had a huge crush on a boy named Bruce Bouwman when I was in eighth grade and he was a senior. Bruce was tall and had dreamy brown eyes. He also had the most beautiful singing voice of anyone at Jasper High School, perhaps in its history. Sadly, he had no idea who I was beyond that I was my older sister's little sister. I had no name.

Common Ground

When I wore my junior high basketball cheerleading outfit to school on game days and went out of my way to walk past his locker, he never noticed me. Even though I went to every performance of *Oklahoma!* (he played Curly, of course) and all his choir concerts, and I had a front-row seat at homecoming coronation, he still didn't notice me. He graduated and went to college, my family moved to Minneapolis, and that, I thought, was the end of it.

Four years later, I spent the summer after my high school graduation in Jasper, staying (mostly) with my grandmother. In June, a group of friends and I had tickets to see Styx in Sioux Falls. I broke my foot earlier in the week (a little mishap in a bowling alley) and needed to use crutches for a few days. The concert was general admission and my friends planned to stand close to the stage. I knew with crutches that would be next to impossible. Luckily (and so random), the day before the concert, I ran into Curt, who I remembered from church, who said he was going to the concert with his friends, too, and they planned to sit in the stands. Seeing my predicament, he said he'd save me a seat.

At the concert, my friend Lisa helped me find Curt. She'd gone to the same church as me and knew Curt vaguely, too, so she knew who I was looking for. When we found him, I settled in while he and Lisa exchanged hellos. I scoped out the surroundings. Curt was at the end of a line of nine guys I kind of recognized, all of whom were older than me, but it was the one sitting next to him who made my heart stop for a minute.

"Who is that next to you?" I whispered in Curt's ear.

"Bruce Bouwman," he said.

"That's Bruce Bouwman!" I squeaked in Lisa's ear.

About that time, Bruce was whispering in Curt's other ear.

"Who's that girl?" he asked.

"Lynn Haraldson. You know, Debbie's little sister," said Curt.

"*That's* Debbie's little sister?" Obviously he noticed I'd outgrown puberty and was sans orthodontia.

I tried to concentrate on the concert, but all I could think about was Bruce. Apparently, all he could think about was me, too, because a few days later, he greeted me with a huge grin when he saw me walking, well, crutching down the sidewalk in downtown Jasper. He was sitting on the hood of his friend's car wearing a cowboy hat, cowboy boots, jeans, and a yellow polo shirt. I was having a good hair day.

"We're going to Granny Kindt's," he said.

"So are we."

"So, I'll see you out there?"

"Absolutely."

Granny Kindt lived on a farm and her grandsons threw parties there, large and small. She loved having "the young folks" out at her house, and everyone loved her. Bruce and Curt went to the party with their friend, Brian, and I'd driven my car with a few of my friends in tow. Bruce and I convinced Brian to drive my friends back to town after the party, and Bruce, Curt and I went back to Curt's farm where I made us scrambled eggs, bacon, and toast. I don't remember what we talked about, but it felt an awful lot like the night before Christmas. I was full of anticipation and had all those wonderful butterflies floating in my stomach.

Around 4 a.m., I drove Bruce back to his car in town. He said there was another party the next night and asked if I wanted to go. Yes, I did, and he leaned over and kissed me lightly on the lips; no tongue, no other body parts touching, just the most beautiful kiss ever.

Update: When Bruce and I got married, Curt was Bruce's best man and Lisa was my maid of honor. Eighteen months later, Curt and Lisa were married. They have four children and still live on a farm outside of Jasper.

Common Ground

A Mother's Day Story
Posted May 2000

Growing up, many of my friends lived on farms, and I sometimes helped out with a chore or two. Not enough to understand the inner workings of farm life, but enough to think I did.

At our grocery store, milk and meat were already packaged when they reached the unloading dock, so I never thought about all the messy stuff in between farm and store until I married a farmer. As naively as humanly possible, I thought it would be fun to raise cows and pigs. After all, I owned a dog once.

Married in the spring of 1982, Bruce and I lived a Normal Rockwell painting into fall. Bruce taught me to drive a tractor, a skid loader, and a three-on-the-tree Ford pickup. I held one-day-old piglets while Bruce gave them iodine shots and cut their eyeteeth, and then returned them to their mothers. All summer, we fed cattle, bailed hay, and watched the calves, pigs, corn, and soybeans grow.

Summer turned into autumn. The soybeans and corn dried in the fields, and the piglets had grown too big to slide under the gate to play in the yard. They spent their days in a wooden building with hay beds and a concrete outdoor yard, separate from the sows. Bruce explained that soon the calves, too, would be separated from their mothers. I didn't fully grasp what that implied until early one October morning, Bruce's father, brother, and nephew came to the farm to wean and sterilize the calves. They made me the gatekeeper. Bruce and his father drove our old three-on-the-tree into the pasture followed by his brother and nephew on three-wheelers, and our dog, Duke. I closed the gate and waited, bouncing up and down to stay warm. Geese flew overhead. The sound of combines harvesting beans hummed softly in the distance. The wind rustled through the drying cornfields. Crows disappeared into the stalks.

Then, all hell broke loose.

Bruce raced up in the truck, followed by two hundred running and confused cows and calves. He slammed on the brakes and got out of the truck. He and the dog separated the calves and moved them toward the gate while his father, brother, and nephew kept the cows back. I opened the gate and guided the calves through the yard. Bruce shut the gate, and the cows paced back and forth along the fence, raising their heads and bellowing.

By the time I walked to the stockyard, my brother-in-law was already clamping the male calves' legs between iron rails. Systematically, he cut off their scrotums and tossed them to the dog. My father-in-law, armed with large pruning shears, cut off the little nubs of horns growing on their foreheads as Bruce held them steady. The calves' eyes were wild, and they tossed and bucked in their confinement as drops of blood trickled down their face. Once released, they huddled against the fence and bawled to their mothers.

The cows' wailing was deafening, and it continued throughout the night. I lay awake thinking about what we'd done. I was four months pregnant and I whispered to Bruce that no one would come after me in a pickup truck to separate me from our baby. He mumbled something about how it was impossible to compare a human with a cow. I silently disagreed.

When I went outside to start chores the next morning, a few cows were still able to cry, their voices hoarse and strained. I walked past the stockyard where the newly orphaned calves stood apart from the calves that had been weaned the year before. They were silent, standing in the dirt, their big eyes following me as I disappeared into the silo room. For a moment I thought about opening the gates and letting them run to their mothers. Instead, I opened two fifty-pound bags of pellets and added them to the silage pouring into the trough.

Winter was quiet. Chores and fixing equipment for spring planting filled most of our time, until a day in mid-February, when we were reminded how nature loves her little surprises.

It was late afternoon. The sun would set soon. Our pregnant cows plodded through the snow, bellies swaying, to the south side of the pasture where there was more protection from the north wind. The pasture shared a fence with the stockyard, but neither the cows or their calves acknowledged one another. Bruce was scooping hay with the tractor for their evening meal.

On my way to church that morning, I'd seen a cow walking away from the herd and I forgot to mention it to Bruce. Now, in the near twilight, I saw two figures in the distance. It was the wandering cow with a tiny red calf. She stopped every few feet, waiting patiently while her calf took his first steps through the snow. She called to him. He answered with a tiny voice.

I flagged down Bruce and he turned off the tractor.

"Look," I said, pointing to the pair. We watched them in silence for a moment before he said it was too cold for the calf to be outside. He opened the gate to the pasture and told me to keep it open while he went to get them. I reminded him I was eight months pregnant. I could barely walk, let alone run, and if ninety seven pregnant bovines wanted out, I wasn't going to stop them. He laughed and walked out into the pasture.

Alone at the gate, the cows and I stared at each other. I touched my belly through my parka. The baby kicked my ribs and rolled over my bladder. I wondered what it felt like to carry around ninety pounds of child rather than nine, or to sleep out in the cold and snow instead of next to a warm body under a quilt. Bruce's yelling yanked me from my daydream, his arms filled with the red calf and one angry mother in pursuit.

When they were through the gate, I slammed it shut and watched as the cow tried to run over Bruce. She bellowed for her calf.

"I'm not stealing your baby!" Bruce yelled back to her.

'But you will,' I thought. 'We steal them every year.'

The Pause
Posted March 10, 2014

Thirty-one years ago today was my daughter's due date, only she wasn't interested in being born just yet. According to his measuring tape and his best guess, my doctor said Carlene weighed in excess of eight pounds and that she wouldn't be born for another few weeks if she had her way.

"Your blood pressure is high, the baby is big enough," he said, taking off his gloves. "We need to get the baby out."

"Ok," I said, like I knew what he meant.

He left the room, I got dressed, and a nurse came in with some papers. She told me I had to check into the hospital.

"Ok," I said. Again, I asked no questions because I was nineteen years old and I was stuck between the fear of the unknown and the mandate by which I was raised: never question authority.

I walked numbly to the waiting area. Bruce met me near the coat rack.

"So, what did he say?" he asked cheerfully, helping me into my coat. Bruce was terribly excited to meet the baby. Every night, he rubbed my belly like it was Aladdin's lamp. "Come out and play!" he'd say.

"I have to go to the hospital," I said quietly, trying not to cry. "He said the baby has to be born soon."

He took my hand and I clutched the papers with the other. We walked to the parking lot and Bruce helped me into the car. Nothing was easy anymore.

Bruce slid into the driver's seat. I looked over the papers the nurse had given me and could feel my heart pulsing in my temples.

"I don't know what any of this means!" I slapped the papers. "I don't know what they're going to do. Am I having a C-section? Is the baby OK?"

Bruce took a deep breath. "Let's just sit here for a minute," he said.

"But they're expecting us at the hospital! We have to go!" I cried. God knows I had to do exactly what I was told at the exact moment I was told to do it.

"They'll be there when we get there," he said softly. He reached over and stroked my hair. "We need some time to think."

So we paused. I took a deep breath and loosened my death grip on the papers. I was afraid and so was he, but we were afraid together. When we felt ready to go, as was always Bruce's positive approach to life, he said, "We're having a baby!" Which we did, the next day, at 7:27 in the evening after more than thirteen hours of labor. No C-section.

Carlene Rae came out looking just like her father, and as she grew, she took on his nature, even though they only knew each other for eleven days. Like her father, Carlene prefers to take her time, and she chafes against the hectic world and deadlines. She's the person you want holding your hand when you're shaking and uncertain, and she will remind you, with a joyful heart, about the good stuff yet to come.

Anger: His
Posted July 2007

By the summer of 1986, JR had been angry with me many times for reasons too small to remember, so I don't recall why he was pacing in our bedroom.

"Do you want to grill pork chops for dinner?" I called down the hallway.

"No!" he yelled, and put his fist through the wall.

Sometimes he raised his hand in front of my face in a Ralph Kramden "Why I oughta..." kind of way, which scared me a little, but I always managed to smooth things over. Feeding him beer usually worked. Vodka even better.

But this was a first, this pacing and punching walls. I was in the kitchen, standing between the refrigerator and the counter. Cassie, eighteen-months old, was bouncing in her yellow high chair attached to the table, banging her little metal spoon on her bowl and singing. Carlene was visiting Bruce's parents for the week. My brother, Matthew, lived with us, but he wasn't home from work.

I called down the hall, "What's wrong?" and he punched a second hole in the wall. I was afraid my face would be next, or worse, the baby's, so I grabbed Cassie and my purse and got in my car. As I drove away, JR screamed out the front door, "You fucking bitch!" and I remember thinking, *Thank God he didn't call me fat.*

When Bruce died in 1983, I didn't let my world crumble, as maybe I should have for a while. Instead, I quickly built a new life, one of sand and straw, in an effort to pardon myself from what felt like an emotional death sentence.

Widowed at nineteen, my only role models were women like my grandmothers who watched Lawrence Welk and played Canasta on Saturday nights, knitted bathroom tissue holder covers, and drank Mogen David on special occasions. They didn't talk to men, especially widowers. Once a week they went to the senior center and ate meatloaf, mashed potatoes, and canned corn, and sat cloistered in the same pews at church every Sunday. They never drove after dark.

Marrying again so soon after Bruce died absolved me of widowhood, and even though it wasn't a very good marriage, at least I wasn't alone. JR distracted me from grief, and walking on the eggshells that was our marriage took a lot of concentration.

When the domestic violence began in July 1986, I was overweight, but I didn't want to know what I weighed. If I did, I'd feel compelled to diet, and food was my emotional crutch. Food didn't threaten me or yell at me. It was reliably comfortable, an unwitting good friend. I didn't have to pacify it or boost its ego. It was there solely for me. A late-night ham and cheese sandwich made me sleepy. An Egg McMuffin (or two) and a couple of hash browns on my way to work helped me focus. If I knew my weight, I'd lose the one thing that didn't judge me.

The morning after the first violent episode, I went home to inspect the damage once I was certain JR had gone to work. There was a three-inch stab mark through the front door, which I assumed was from the butcher knife he'd threatened my brother with when he got home from work. JR had also put his fist through the front window.

The same kind of numbness that shrouded me when I learned Bruce had died wrapped me in its care as I looked around my house that had been raped by anger. Violence didn't fit inside the box that was my reality. I was a wife and mother of two children. I lived in the suburbs. I had a car payment and a job. I went "up north" on summer weekends like everyone else in Minneapolis. I had HBO and Showtime. Holes in walls and stab marks in doors were so far beyond wrong they were beyond my comprehension. I didn't know what else to do except put on the radio and begin sweeping up the glass.

JR called while I was cleaning. He said he was sorry. He said it wouldn't happen again. I said OK, but I moved the knives from the storage block on the counter to the silverware drawer, just in case.

I hung pictures over the holes in the bedroom and our landlord replaced the window after I told him one of the girls had accidently thrown a ball through it. I couldn't do anything about the stab mark in the door, but we rarely used the front door anyway, so I didn't notice them again until JR tried to push me out of the house a few months later.

While there'd been no new threats, the tension between us was palpable. I wanted us to separate without causing World War III, but he was a live grenade and it wouldn't have mattered if I asked him for a kiss or a divorce. Something would make him explode, and drinking vodka on the night I decided to deliver my news was definitely not my most stellar decision.

It was a Saturday night, the weekend before Thanksgiving. The kids were asleep and JR was watching TV. He'd been eerily quiet and it was that eerie silence that always scared me the most. That night, however, his silence pushed me to the point of enough. I was done. No more living in fear (so said the vodka)!

I sat down a few feet away and looked at him. His legs were stretched out across the ottoman and crossed at the ankles. His arms were folded at his chest, and he held a beer in his right hand. His once beautiful blue eyes were dark and cold, staring straight ahead at the television.

"I want a divorce," I said matter-of-factly. "I'm going to take the kids and stay with my parents for a few days." He turned his head slowly and gave me "the look." He said nothing.

I stood up and went to the kitchen to call my mother. When she answered, I asked if the kids and I could spend the night. Before she could say anything, JR came up behind me and ripped the phone off the wall.

"You're not taking my kids anywhere," he said through a clenched jaw. He grabbed me by my shirt collar and dragged me to the front door. I heard the basement phone ring.

It snowed that day, but being out in the cold didn't worry me. I couldn't let him lock me out of the house for fear of what he'd do to the girls.

"I'm not leaving without them," I said coolly. I wrestled out of his grip and ran toward the hallway. He ran after me and dragged me back to the front door. Again, I got away, and again he came after me and pinned me against the kitchen wall. Except for our breathing, the room was quiet. JR's glassy eyes stared into mine and I didn't look away. I couldn't let him win.

A knock on the side door stopped whatever was coming next.

"Lynnie, it's Dad." He spoke in the voice he used when he read books to me when I was a child. "I brought along a few friends. Can you open the door?"

JR loosened his grip and yelled something like go away, that this was his property. I slipped away and ran down the hallway to Cassie's room. I grabbed her out of her crib and fled to Carlene's room. I popped a Sesame Street tape into Carlene's tape recorder and ironically, "In Harmony" came on. I cranked up the volume and nearly threw the girls in the closet, closing the door just before the police broke down the side door.

The police dragged JR out of the house without his coat and shoes and put him in jail for the weekend. On Monday, they let him out. He called and said he was sorry. He said it wouldn't happen again. He said he had nowhere to go. I knew I'd be financially strapped without him, and more than that, I was afraid if he didn't come back, no one would ever love me again. He completed a court-ordered anger management class and quit drinking. Two months later, he moved home.

Anger: Mine
Posted July 2007

Three in the morning on a hot July night, 1987. My mother, sister, and I were watching Mickey Mouse cartoons in a hospital waiting room, anxious for news about Dad, who'd suffered a heart attack. I was reclined sideways in a chair, my legs dangling over the arm when my stomach started to churn. The feeling crept upward to my heart, which began beating wildly. Then it went to my lungs and I couldn't complete a full breath. It finally settled in my mind and I thought, 'I'm dying!' Within a few minutes, I was on a gurney in the emergency room and a doctor was handing me a pill.

"You had a panic attack," he said. "Here, put this under your tongue."

It was Halcion. Valium with a kick, and now illegal in England. Within seconds, I was calm. So calm I forgot why I was at the hospital. My sister reminded me as she poured me into the front seat of my car to take me home. I remember saying, "Oh, that's right," and drifted off to sleep.

I slept the rest of the morning. When I woke up, I felt like I'd been hit by a truck. I was groggy and deeply frightened. Did my heart just skip? Why can't I breathe? The panic had returned and my only defense was to slip another Halcion under my tongue.

Panic came back the next day and the next. By the end of the week, my defenses were spent. The pill bottle was empty.

The next two weeks, panic poured over me like a tsunami. I went to every emergency room in the Minneapolis area begging for relief, usually in the middle of the night, waking JR and dragging the kids out from their beds because I couldn't drive myself. The last ER physician I saw said I needed to see a psychiatrist and refused to write a script. He sent me home shaking and throwing up.

So I called a psychiatrist. He wanted to explore my past. I just wanted drugs. He assured me I could control my panic through deep breathing. I told him I hadn't caught my breath in weeks. He still refused me drugs.

A few days later, my IBM Selectric II typewriter ribbon broke at work and I began to cry. I cried while I changed it, cried as I typed a memo, and cried when my boss sent me home because I couldn't stop crying. I cried driving home, cried while I made and ate a grilled cheese sandwich, and I cried as I dialed the phone to tell my psychiatrist I was crying. I cried even harder when he told me he was checking me in to the hospital. A special hospital.

A few hours later, JR dropped me off at the front doors, and I checked in to the psychiatric ward. I'd stopped crying, but I was exhausted. My head felt like a bowling ball, and I answered questions with monosyllabic words.

After filling out insurance forms, a nurse led me to a scale in the hallway across from the nurses' station. I was wearing knee-length knit shorts and a size XXL t-shirt stained at the hem. Tears had washed away my makeup, and my hair was matted to my head. I took off my slip-on canvas shoes with the hole in the toe and laid them beside the scale. The nurse optimistically started the large metal weight at the one-hundred-pound position and nudged the smaller weight higher and higher. The balance arrow didn't budge. She moved the large weight to two hundred and again moved the small weight higher. The arrow bounced a little around two hundred forty. For accuracy, she should have moved the large weight to two hundred fifty, but she said cheerfully, "We'll call you two forty nine."

The next day, I spent two hours in group therapy drawing pictures and writing in a journal and feeling completely out of place and ridiculously selfish among people facing electric shock therapy. One woman was the only survivor of a car crash that killed her niece and sister. She'd been the driver. A chain-smoking young man had locked himself in a closed garage and started his car's engine a few weeks before. He'd been repeatedly molested as a child.

I thought, 'Can I be a bigger baby?' as I wrote my name with a blue crayon on a piece of yellow construction paper. We were to draw a "family tree of feelings." The only thing I felt was guilty for taking up space in a facility meant for people with real problems, and stupid for having called my doctor in the first place. So I'd cried for a few hours? Big deal. People cry.

I took a two-hour, fill-in-the-hole-with-a-number-two-pencil psychological test that asked me to answer yes or no to statements such as, "I would like to do the work of a choir director" and "If I could sneak into the county fair or an amusement park without paying, I would." Were they kidding me?

The next day, a psychiatrist went over my results. She showed me a line chart indicating how I "scored" in regard to various emotions and behaviors. The line was flowing along nicely, indicating I was "normal" here and "normal" there, just as I expected. Then a steep, jagged line rose across the paper like a fjord on the Norwegian coastline. It went all the way to the top of the chart before plummeting back to the middle.

"That's your anger line," the doctor said.

"What?" I laughed. "Just because I don't want to be a choir director, I'm angry? I have nothing to be angry about!"

I explained that I had a panic disorder, and told her how a few days ago I couldn't stop crying and that was why I was there. I just needed to calm down, maybe lose some weight. I'd be fine.

She nodded, wrote a few notes, and gave me Xanax. I promised to visit my psychiatrist weekly for a month and was released from the facility at the end of the week.

The Xanax worked almost instantly, and it kept the physical symptoms of anxiety at bay. But the relentless weeks-long waves of panic prior to the Xanax made me afraid of fear, and I was scared that I'd have another attack at any moment. I needed something to change, something to help me feel normal again. God knows my psychiatrist was no help. He read the hospital psychiatrist's report and ran with her whole "anger" diagnosis. He wanted me to journal about my anger, even though I insisted I wasn't angry. But in order to get the Xanax, I wrote in the journal.

He brought up Bruce's death and asked me about my current husband, who in the past had been physically and emotionally violent, but I wouldn't go there with him. All was forgiven. There was nothing I could do to change the past, so why dwell on it? He said something about unresolved grief and lack of self-esteem and blah blah blah.

'Buddy,' I thought, 'all I want is some control of my life.'

I discovered the golden loophole a few weeks later when I went to my gynecologist for a routine exam. I told her how anxious I'd been feeling, leaving out the part about the hospital and the psychiatrist, and she diagnosed me with severe PMS. She wrote me a script for Xanax and that was the end of journaling about non-existent anger. I focused my energy on the one thing I knew I could control: my weight.

I joined Weight Watchers, but not before saying goodbye to a few of my "friends," the ones I knew I wouldn't be able to "contact" once I was on a diet.

The week before the first meeting, I made macaroni and cheese with real butter, and I grilled a T-bone steak. I ate garlic mashed potatoes and cheesy hash browns, baked a chocolate cake, and went twice to Dairy Queen for a Hot Fudge Brownie Delight. I poured two-percent milk over Captain Crunch for breakfast, and made a parade of pasta dishes for dinner. Then on Saturday morning, after throwing out the leftover brie and French baguette, deviled eggs, and Hershey Kisses, I walked into a Weight Watchers facility, paid the eight-dollar fee, weighed in and left without attending the meeting. After four weeks, I'd acquired all the basic program materials and stopped going.

"You'll leave me once you've lost weight," JR said.

"No, I won't!" I insisted.

I subsisted on raw and boiled vegetables, fruit, skim milk, and plain baked white fish. In my WW food journal, I checked off every allotted carb, protein, and dairy allowed. I ate nothing more. I quit drinking and started riding a stationary bike I bought at a garage sale for ten dollars. In return, I averaged a three-pound loss every week.

I wasn't angry. Heck no. Just highly motivated.

Update: JR and I divorced a year later, yet I continued running away from my anger and anxiety for nine more years, always looking for shortcut solutions and substitutes for therapy. Finally, on a summer day in 1996, after living in Pennsylvania for five years and having been married and divorced again, I decided I was done. I went to a sporting goods store and put ten percent down on a handgun. I filled out the background check paperwork and the clerk said I could pick up the gun in two days.

I drove to my favorite spot by the Clarion River. For an hour, I hated on myself and I cried for my losses and the stupid decisions I'd made over the years. Then I remembered my children. They were just up the hill from the river, in our apartment, completely unaware their mother was thinking of leaving them in a most violent way.

I went home, made an appointment with a psychologist, and didn't complete the gun purchase.

Today, I still have anxiety and I take lorazepam when needed. I also meditate almost daily. I know people who treat anxiety and panic attacks as character flaws and believe that if they were just "strong enough" they wouldn't suffer as they do. Please, I'm begging you, if this is you, stop beating yourself up. Talk to your doctor. And if that doctor says it's all in your head, talk to another doctor. Keep talking until you get the help you need.

Running Naked Through a Graveyard
Posted March 2007

Leave it to my Grandma Signe to die on a leap day, February 29, 1996.

Unusual is too strong a word to describe a woman who chewed gum with her front teeth, but to me, my grandma was eccentric for keeping a small bottle of Southern Comfort in her refrigerator.

Signe had an Andy Warhol eye for color, and was a slipper knitter and a first-rate doily maker. A coterie of widows were her loyal companions. She drove a big green boat of a Chevy, and with her right foot on the gas and her left foot on the brake (usually at the same time), and on Thursdays, she'd pick up her friends and road trip five blocks to the senior center for potluck and gossip.

Signe never forgot to send a card and a couple of bucks for every grandchild's birthday, and when she came to visit, she always played games and talked to us about us, never about herself. She was careful to stay away from stories about her past. It's as though she didn't have one, like she was always a grandma, never a girl. To me, Signe was born at age sixty and simply grew older as I did.

We all have defining moments in our lives, some more difficult than others. Signe's was when her husband Martin died. She was thirty three and eight months pregnant. My dad, also named Martin, was six.

When Martin died, Signe never spoke his name again, and insisted my dad be called by his middle name, Donald. Maybe she didn't see the point in talking about something she couldn't change, but I suspect she loved Martin so much that his death knocked the wind out of her, and the only way she found to breathe again was to not talk about it.

Signe and Martin grew up on farms just a few miles from each other. She went to college and eventually taught school a half mile from Martin's homestead. They dated for many years, marrying in December 1930. My father was born in February 1931. You do the math.

Martin was good friends with Signe's siblings, and was known around the area as the guy with the fancy car with a canvas top and side curtains.

Signe was never an overly-talkative person, but she was no wallflower. She had a way of letting you know you did something she didn't like. My dad's memories of his father are few, but clear. He told me how one day, Signe poured Martin a cup of coffee. When it was full enough, Martin yelled, "Whoa!" Signe kept right on pouring, letting the coffee spill over the cup and onto the table. She said curtly, "Don't you talk to me like you do your horses."

It never happened again.

Maybe her refusal to speak of Martin seems strange in our modern world of readily available therapy and support groups. But in 1937, a farmer's widow with two small children didn't have much time to feel everything she was feeling, let alone cry or talk about it. My guess is she simply shut off those emotions and went on with the business of raising her children in a world wary of single mothers.

Signe obtained a loan to buy a house, which she fixed up as a boarding house for single female school teachers. For extra money, she made donuts and sent my dad down the street selling them for two bits a dozen. He never got more than three blocks from home before running out.

During World War II, she went back to the classroom, teaching school until she retired twenty years later.

Signe's parents moved in when they retired from farming, and from then on Signe kept busy with choir and Bible study and playing cards with her friends. Apparently, Signe's mother griped about her never being home, but if you knew my great-grandmother, you'd hardly blame Signe for getting out once in a while.

And that's how I knew Signe, as a woman who got out once in a while.

Toward the end of her life, Signe suffered from dementia. She said some things that, in more lucid moments, she would never have said. But with dementia, she no longer lived in the present, as she had since Martin died. Her past was all she had. She spoke of her parents, her siblings, her friends, and of running naked through a graveyard.

I mean no disrespect to my grandmother, but I hope a long time ago she did run through a cemetery, carefree, happy, beautiful, and spontaneous. I hope the last few years, weeks, and hours of her life were filled with the thoughts she spent all her life trying to forget. Warm, wonderful thoughts of how much she loved and was loved.

Lutefisk
Posted December 2007

I have the best dad in the whole world for a lot of reasons, but one puts him over the top. Among all the boxes shipped to my house from an array of online retail outlets this week, one was from Broton, Minnesota, marked PERISHABLE, and I knew exactly what that meant: The ambrosia had arrived. All the other boxes could wait on the porch. PERISHABLE from Broton was urgent.

The one-pound package of lutefisk had defrosted in shipping, but was still cold. Not that cold or not cold matters much. You can do pretty much anything you want to lutefisk. Freeze, defrost, refreeze, hang it outside on a clothes line. It'll taste pretty much the same once you cook it.

Translated, lutefisk means "lye fish." It is dried cod that is, literally, soaked in water and lye for several days. The fish is then soaked for several more days in cold water to eliminate the lye. The lutefisk that arrived from Broton had already been de-lyed and was ready to cook.

Even though each year, hundreds of people stand in line for hours to eat lutefisk at Lutheran churches hosting lutefisk dinners, most people I know in Minnesota don't like...no, wait, they downright *hate*... the gelatinous consistency and taste, and they make lutefisk the butt of many jokes. But sticks and stones, my friends. Sticks and stones.

Dad was my lutefisk dinner partner until I moved to Pennsylvania. Now I eat my lutefisk alone. It's not that we talked much when we ate. You don't *talk* when you eat lutefisk except to say, "Please pass the lutefisk" or potatoes or lefse or butter or sugar (for the lefse). We were united in our cause, two lutefisk soldiers fighting the onslaught of insults hurled at us from our loved ones. My mother was the worst. Every year she'd snidely insinuate that the barbecue ribs or eggplant parmesan or chicken Kiev she made was superior to our "stinky old lutefisk" (her words, not mine). "It smells like an armpit," others said, but my dad and I ignored them and kept on eating, confident in our consumption, delirious in our butter coma.

This week, my stepsons will help me make lefse to go with my lutefisk. No one in my Pennsylvania family likes lutefisk, but everyone loves lefse. Lefse this and lefse that. Sure, it's good. I love it, too. But during a lutefisk dinner, its purpose is to scoop lutefisk on to your fork, kind of like bread at a roast beef dinner. Lutefisk is the featured act. Lefse is the warm-up band.

I will prepare my lutefisk dinner after everyone and their negativity has gone back to work and school. I will cook it, slap some butter and sugar on a few lefse rounds, boil up some white potatoes, and sit down at my dining room table, alone, with a photo of my father by my side. I will eat my lutefisk in peace. No insults, no talking. Just me and my all-white-food feast.

Summer Vacation
Posted August 2008

My flight arrived in Minneapolis at dawn on Sunday, and I wandered, bleary-eyed, around the underbelly of the airport for an hour in search of the right rental car counter. I'd reserved a practical car to get me from family to family for a week, but when Budget put me behind the wheel of a cherry red Dodge Caliber loaded with Sirius satellite radio and a sunroof, I was on a *real* vacation.

I pulled out of the parking garage, cranked up Classic Rewind, opened the sunroof, and let my hair blow straight up in the air. It was already stinky hot and humid, and I loved it.

The sunroof is why I'm writing this from Lake Edward in central Minnesota instead of locked in my hotel room writing, as was my plan. My family had gone there for a few days, and I confess I missed them as much as I wanted to drive the car again. I called my daughter and told her I was packing the Caliber and heading to the lake. I checked out of the hotel, put on my shades, and hit the highway.

I haven't seen a decent sunset since the last time I was in Minnesota. Sunsets in Pennsylvania, while pretty, are brief. The sun disappears behind the hills and trees long before it sets. Here on the prairie, you watch the sun slowly sink in the western sky like a pancake absorbing thick syrup. As I watched the long, lazy sunset between Big Lake and St. Cloud, I knew I'd made the right decision to leave my work unwritten.

It was dark when I arrived. Claire was already in bed. The rest of us sat on the deck in short sleeves and t-shirts, except Carlene, who looked like Eminem curled up in her sweat pants with a hoodie pulled over her head. Mosquitoes are on that girl like flies on stink. I don't know if it's her neon white skin or if she has better blood than the rest of us, but there isn't a mosquito in the state that doesn't know when Carlene's in town.

I was up early this morning, awakened by a hummingbird outside the screen window next to the couch where I was sleeping. Baby Claire is awake and rummaging through my suitcase. My parents are talking on the deck. My brother is making eggs and bacon. He'll soon get the boat ready for a morning of fishing with Dad and my son-in-law. There isn't a cloud in the sky and the lake is sparkling.

Moments like this don't happen holed up in a hotel room. They come compliments of a rental car sunroof and an impractical inner voice that says, "Let's go!"

Lynn Haraldson

***

From Lake Edward, I drove to Jasper in southwest Minnesota for the Jasper High School All-School Reunion and Goat Races. Yes, goat races, but that's not the strange part of this story.

I was staying at my cousin's farm for the weekend. When I arrived, two older women were getting out of a car in front of the house. Thinking they were extended family in town for the reunion, I introduced myself.

"Hi, I'm Lynn. Don's daughter." I smiled and extended my hand.

One of the women reluctantly shook it and looked with concern at the other woman.

"I'm looking for Dean," she said.

"Oh. I'm sorry," I said. "He's in Pipestone with his son. He'll be home in an hour."

"Well, we're burying my brother tomorrow and I need to drop him off with Dean."

After an uncomfortable moment of silence, she continued. "He's in the trunk."

I knew Dean mowed the cemetery across the road, but I had no idea he was the grave digger, too.

"Well, OK," I said, after what she said settled in my mind. "I guess you should bring him in the house, then."

I assumed she wasn't going to whip out a casket, but I admit I was relieved when she opened the trunk and the two women lifted out a medium sized cardboard box. I held open the back door, and when they were inside, I looked desperately around the kitchen.

"You can set him down...um...there," I said, pointing to a space on the floor next to the microwave cabinet. They set down the box, said a terse thank you, and walked out the door.

I stood there for a moment looking at the box. I called Dean and got his voicemail.

"I have no idea who this guy is, but he's in a box on your kitchen floor," I said at the beep. "Welcome home to me...I think?"

* * *

The Transportation Safety Authority apparently gets suspicious of luggage containing a hand weight, tennis ball, a lacy pink thong, and Trader Joe's corn tortilla crackers. When I opened my checked bag when I got back to Pennsylvania, there was a note inside that said, in essence, "X-ray showed you travel with some weird shit, lady, so we opened your bag and dug around. Sorry if we packed it back up wrong. Hugs and kisses, TSA."

Minnesota was hot and sunny, just the way I remembered. Except for a few mosquito bites on my rear end (I swear I was clothed in public the entire time) and a few mysterious bruises, I suffered no injuries and had no scrapes with the car, something I always worry about when I'm driving a rental.

Maybe it's true that you can't go home again and expect it to be the same. But sometimes it's good to go home again to remember where you came from.

I drank Bud Light while riding in a parade on a flatbed with friends from my graduating class. While I had moved in ninth grade and graduated from another school, I consider Jasper High School my alma mater. Carlene joined us, which gave her a weird kind of insight into what I was like during my Jasper High days.

I reminisced with my sixth-grade boyfriend, and hung out with my junior high cheerleading squad and the other member of the flute section.

Carlene met the woman she's named after, a good friend of her father, who is named, of course, Carlene. She also met Bruce's and my former choir director, Bruce's second grade teacher, and a few more of

Bruce's friends, all of whom were blown away by how much she looks and sounds like her father.

I slept in eight beds in nine nights, and every day, something reminded me of what I love about Minnesota, and, to be honest, the reasons I choose to live in Pennsylvania. It's mostly because of the winter weather, but there are ghosts in Minnesota that are best left there, where I can visit them once in a while rather than live among them.

Marty
Posted June/July 2011

On Thursday, after I got home from a rainy bike ride, my brother Matthew called to tell me that our brother Marty had suffered the mother of all grand mal seizures. It happened as he was getting ready for work around 6:30 or 7:00 in the morning, but living alone, no one found him until noon.

Marty's history with brain injuries and epilepsy began in 1971 when he was eighteen and on a missions trip to Puerto Rico. A van he was riding in crashed and Marty was thrown from the van and knocked unconscious. He was in a coma for three days.

A few years later, Marty started to experience vacant moments in which you could wave your hand in front of his face and he would be completely unaware. His eyes were cold and empty, like he was dead with his eyes open. We know now that he was having petit mal seizures, but at the time, he didn't seek medical help. He just called them his "ghosts," and they scared the hell out of him.

During the Des Moines flood in 1993, Marty went to help bag sand and clean the debris left by the flood waters. A few days after he got home, he developed meningitis, which almost killed him.

A year later, he had his first grand mal seizure. He woke up on his bedroom floor, his head bloodied from hitting the nightstand. It took several months and seizures for his doctors to fine-tune his medications, and once they did, Marty was able to drive again, return to the job he loved, and enjoy a fairly normal life, despite chronic headaches.

Thursday's seizure wasn't like the others. The post-ictal period (the time during which the brain recovers from a seizure) lasted several hours, and it was the next day before he recognized anyone. Five days later, he still has no sense of time, and yesterday, he couldn't remember the words "blue jeans" when Matthew asked him what he wanted him to bring him from his house.

Marty is aware, however, of his feelings, and the feeling he's experiencing most is sadness.

"I feel so low," he told Matthew.

Marty is one of the most positive people I know. In nearly forty years, he's never let his epilepsy or headaches get him down. Living a thousand miles away from him, I can't hug him, and I can't even call him. I can only hear about him through my family. I offered to fly out, but Matthew assured me there was nothing I could do right now.

I went on another bike ride today and wouldn't you know it? It began to rain. When I got back to the car, wouldn't you know it? There was a message from Matthew. Marty's doctors found a shadow on the part of his brain that affects memory. They're going to do a spinal tap this afternoon to find out if the shadow is due to an infection. Matthew said the doctors are hoping for an infection because an infection can be cured.

***

Marty's short-term memory is still pretty messed up, but he's made more than a few people smile with his phone calls. He called his boss yesterday to tell him he wouldn't be in to work because he was in the hospital. His boss is who found Marty unconscious in his house the day of his seizure. Marty also called our parents to tell them, too, even though they've been to the hospital several times. He attempted to call Matthew, only he inadvertently called my son-in-law Matt. Matt was surprised to hear from Marty, but he let him know who he was and Marty seemed to remember.

I'm trying not to bug Matthew too much for news. I got the hint the other night when he said to me, a little exasperated, "I'll call you, Lynn. I promise. You know I keep you in the loop." Yes, I know, but as the person who has always taken care of family issues in the past, it's not easy to A) live so far away from it; B) trust someone else to do it; and C) wait. As many of you know, I'm not the most patient person in the world.

* * *

Twenty-some years ago, as Marty attempted to make dinner, he called me.

"I made spaghetti, but…"

"You cooked?" I interrupted, nearly dropping the phone.

"I figure I can't eat McDonalds every day," he said. "But how…"

"Hold on, I have to write this date on the calendar. This is bigger than our birthday."

"I'm serious! I made spaghetti. But how do you get the noodles cooked without the water boiling all over the stove?"

Now, my brother is usually a smart guy. Best salesman his employer ever had. He can fix almost anything, and he's so patient that he never swears when he plays golf.

"I'm not sure what you're asking me."

"Well, I kept having to lift the pot off the stove when it boiled over," he said, exasperated.

Silence.

"Why didn't you just turn down the stove?"

Silence.

"Oh."

Silence.

"Yeah."

Silence.

"Man, I'm a bonehead."

We learned last week that Marty has a lesion in the hippocampus region of his brain, which is causing some amnesia. His neurologist outlined his recovery plan, but he'll need some help. I'm heading out to Minnesota to stay with Marty for a few weeks to take him to doctor and therapy appointments, and help him adjust to life with limited short-term memory.

* * *

Hello from my camper bed in the spare room at my brother's house, a place in which the bathroom has never looked or smelled so girlie.

Marty may be forgetful, but he still has an innate sense of quality. He didn't go cheap when he bought this air mattress. Usually when I sleep on these things I wake up flat on the floor. Not this one. Hasn't lost air yet.

We went to the grocery store yesterday and wandered around for an hour. I interjected "Do you like ____?" questions to gauge his taste, but mostly I listened and watched which foods he was drawn to. Later, I will make a list of the foods I recommended and the ones he seemed interested in. This will hopefully help him make better choices when he goes grocery shopping with someone else after I'm gone.

This was also a grocery trip for me. I flew in late Monday, so there was no time to hit a store before hitting the sack. I'd packed some almonds, powdered peanut butter, and a banana that barely survived in anticipation of nothing being in my brother's house for breakfast. I confess I was pretty excited when he gave me the tour of his cupboard and I saw the bag of Frosted Mini Wheats.

I threw my usual foods in the cart—veggies, fruit, Greek yogurt, pita, hummus, veggie burgers—and he bought milk, orange juice, paper plates, plastic cups, and laundry soap. After putting our groceries in the truck, I asked him where the nearest Starbucks was. It took him a few minutes to consider my question, but he said he thought there was one in Target next door. I told him I'd be right back. When I hopped up into the driver's seat of his F-150 with my venti latte, he was staring at the grocery receipt.

"This is the longest receipt I've ever had," he said. "I've never bought garbanzo beans before!"

We went to my parents' house for dinner, and my sister-in-law and niece joined us. A small gathering, but still a social interaction nonetheless, and Marty's first since the seizure. My mother is hard of hearing and so we need to talk loudly for her to hear us. It's something I am used to and can handle, but I'm not the one with a brain injury. I kept a close eye on Marty, who didn't talk much, and quietly asked him from time to time how he was doing and if he needed anything.

I chopped vegetables and cooked chicken for spinach salads. Marty ate a salad and a piece of bread, and Mom surprised him with his favorite dessert, vanilla ice cream and chocolate sauce.

When we got home, he settled into his recliner with a bottle of water and put on the Twins game. I went outside to make a few phone calls. They were short calls because at 7:30, the heat index was still one hundred eighteen degrees and the dew point was a record-breaking eighty two degrees.

When I came back in, Marty got all big brother on me.

"It's hot out there," he said. "You can make your calls in your room and shut the door. It won't offend me. It's OK."

I assured him next time I would, then he suggested I sit down and put my feet up. We spent the next few hours talking and laughing, and when the game was over, I went to my camper bed after brushing my teeth in his girlified bathroom. I decided that if I did nothing else but be here to remind Marty who he is and always has been, then I will have accomplished my goal.

Before going into his room across the hall, Marty stood in my doorway and smiled.

"I know you're missing your family, but I'm glad you're here."

"But you're my family, too, and I want to be here."

"I know," he said, "but I'm still glad you're here."

Epilogue

Since 2011, I've been to Minnesota only three times. In 2013, my boyfriend Jim and I went out so he could meet my parents and brothers. My sister Debbie, who lives in Seattle, was visiting then, too. In January 2016, Carlene, her husband, Jim and I went out when Bruce's mother, Eileen, passed away. Seeing Bruce's family en masse was a bit overwhelming, but several of my friends, including Lisa and Curt, were there for support. I took Jim on a quick tour of Jasper and we went to the cemetery to visit Bruce's grave. There was already a hole dug for Eileen's coffin. Bruce would be to her left and her husband Walt to her right. It felt oddly peaceful staring into that hole of dark prairie dirt, blanketed all around with several inches of fresh snow. If there is such a place as heaven, I know Bruce and Walt were there to welcome her.

Jim and I drove out again in May 2016. My daughters, their families and I were supposed to go "up north" in June 2020 and vacation with my brother Matthew and his wife, but the pandemic interrupted that plan, and I'm unsure when I'll return.

As for Marty, he sold his house in 2014 and moved to a senior living community. He had a job for a few years bagging groceries, but a small stroke left him unable to walk without a walker and he could not continue to work. His short-term memory is still severely limited and he must write dates and appointments down or he will forget. Thankfully, he has not had a seizure since 2011, and he is in good humor most of the time.

2. Grief

"The pain of grief is just as much part of life as the joy of love: it is perhaps the price we pay for love, the cost of commitment."

—Colin Murray Parkes

The Song Remains The Same
Posted March 2011

On Saturday, the world will formally say goodbye to Hank, husband to Shannon and father of Ella, age four. Hank was thirty eight. He had cancer.

Twenty-eight years ago this month, my husband died when his tractor was hit by a train near our farm. Our daughter was eleven days old. Hank and Bruce lived and died differently, but each left behind a daughter and his daughter's mother.

The days before and the day of Bruce's funeral felt much like the days this week—cold and windy; the air damp and heavy.

Except for the moments I escaped to nurse Carlene, the bathroom had been my only refuge, where people left me alone and I could think for ten minutes without making decisions about flowers, cemetery plots, and caskets. On the day of the funeral, I lingered in the shower longer than usual. I wrapped myself in Bruce's thick brown bathrobe and sat cross-legged on the counter, like I always did when Bruce and I got ready for a date or church. He would shave while I put on my makeup, and we'd listen to the radio and talk.

I rubbed foundation on my face and imagined him next to me knotting his tie, something he tried to teach me many times. I turned on the radio and heard the song "I Won't Hold You Back" by Toto. I sang along until I got to the line, "Now that I'm alone it gives me time, to think about the years that you were mine."

I stared in the mirror. Even though for three days people were everywhere and would be for more days to come, I was alone. I'd been watched and worried about like I was a fragile girl with a scarlet "W" stitched on her chest, but no one could share this pain with me. I was a new mother who should have been perfecting nursing, bathing her baby daughter, and sleeping when she slept. Instead, I was eyed and pawed and clung to by grieving masses, people with real grief, but who would go back to their homes where they could ponder this tragedy while I lived it.

It didn't matter that I felt every bit the nursing, bleeding mother I was. Death came with obligations. No one would understand if I stayed home. I turned off the radio and put on the only outfit that fit me other than maternity clothes: a white knit suit I bought in anticipation of Carlene's baptism. I walked out of the bathroom with my chin up and eyes dry. I left Carlene with a neighbor and got into my father's car to ride to the church.

With a thousand sad eyes watching me, I walked down the aisle behind the pall bearers. Almost a year before, many of those same eyes had watched me walk down that same aisle, holding on to my father's arm as Bruce waited for me at the altar, tall and handsome, young and vibrant.

Now he lay dead in a casket covered in a spray of lilies, carnations, and roses with a small red ribbon attached, scrolled with the word "Daddy."

Except for a few muffled cries, the mourning congregation was controlled and dignified, and I was, too. I kept myself together through "Children of the Heavenly Father" by staring at Bruce's casket. I chose the song because I'd introduced Bruce to it a few months earlier when he was looking for something to sing for a solo in church. Bruce could sing a TV commercial and I'd swoon. Over the summer, I learned to play two of my favorite songs on the piano—"Your Song" by Elton John and "Time in a Bottle" by Jim Croce—just so he'd sing them to me.

When the hymn ended, the church was quiet except for the sound of one person weeping. It was my father, fully engaged in shoulder shaking, head-in-hands, inconsolable sobbing.

Dad was six years old when his father died in 1937, and his mother was eight months pregnant. It was the middle of the Depression, and like chocolate, grief was a luxury. There were fields to plow and children to raise. The only way my grandmother could deal with her grief was to bury it. She didn't return to their home, and moved in with her parents. She did not want Grandpa's name spoken. My dad, who was named after his father, was called by his middle name.

He'd lost his father and his name, and now his only grandchild was fatherless, too. The man had earned the right to cry.

I imagined liberating my own pain that way, or by throwing myself on Bruce's casket and wailing. But I didn't want to be known as the woman who lost it at her husband's funeral. My only emotional emancipation was when I kissed my hand and touched his casket when I thought no one was looking, like I was saying goodbye to a clandestine lover.

Now it is Shannon's turn to cry, and in the days, months and years to follow, she will raise Ella and remember Hank. Her life will go on and she'll work and she'll one day smile, but this week? This week will crawl inside and forever be a part of her.

The Forgiveness Train
Posted August 2007

The Great Plains are a seemingly endless stretch of land as far as the eye can see. Its vastness is daunting and powerful like a god, and will make anyone feel small and insignificant standing in a field of rocks and prairie grass. The wind has nowhere to stop and sounds never linger in one place.

I grew up, got married, and was widowed on the prairie before I moved away, and it was twenty five years before I went back to the railroad tracks on the prairie where my husband was killed.

No one would know anyone died there. It's just a ditch like any ditch anywhere. The intersection is a dirt road over a couple of tracks with a stop sign at the approach. This place of death was quiet, as it was years before. A few cows mooed in the distance, a few birds chirped. It was foggy and misting.

I parked ten feet from the tracks and got out of my car. I looked toward what used to be our farm, a half mile across a field and I heard a train whistle several miles north. The sound was faint, like it traveled on the wind, southbound, the same direction the train came when it struck Bruce's tractor. I approached the tracks, took a few photos, and let whatever I needed to feel be felt: regret and sadness, but mostly anger.

Six weeks after Bruce died, I had a dream that we were sitting on the couch in our living room. I asked him how he could be killed by a train while crossing tracks he'd known were there all his life? Bruce answered calmly, "I didn't hear it."

I didn't understand. "How do you not hear a freight train?"

He smiled and said, "I love you. I have to go now," and I woke up.

Looking again at our farm, I wondered if I should stay and wait for the train and watch it pass, recreate in my head the time a similar freight train sent Bruce's tractor reeling and his body crashing through the windshield and into the ditch. Did I want to witness its crossing? Feel its wake? Hear its roar?

I walked back to the car, tossed my camera on the dash, and sat down in the driver's seat. I left the door open. I thought staying might bring me closer to his final moments, maybe offer some peace, and so I waited.

A minute passed. I glanced to the left and watched birds fly out of a field. Then I glanced casually to my right and I sucked in a startled breath. There it was, barreling toward me like the freight train it was. The whistle blew as it approached the intersection, but I didn't hear it coming.

I had barely a second to jump out of my car and take a photo. The ground trembled and the sound was deafening, yet, when it passed, I watched it continue silently on its journey.

I remembered something my friend Rodney wrote to me, about how he felt after his daughter was born: "I remember those heady days, when it seems like you have the world by the tail: a loving wife, a job you love, the home you've always dreamed of and wanted, and especially when a new little baby daughter has entered your life. Well, I remember I felt invincible, like I would live forever and nothing bad could ever touch me.

"I can, I think, get a notion of what was in Bruce's mind and heart that day. On the tractor, which is always a good feeling, all that horsepower at your fingertips, ready to turn the land, pull the harvest. The open air of the countryside, even in the tractor cab. Beautiful young wife at home preparing a meal, your new daughter ready to be held in your hands. I believe when that sudden and tragic end came, Bruce was one of the happiest men on earth."

Years of anger dissolved into compassion as I realized the truth of that awful day: Bruce didn't hear the train. He didn't mean to die.

I looked once more at the farm and thought about the fall nights we spent sitting in a tractor in a field waiting for his brother to bring another load of harvested soybeans; winter nights warming newborn pigs on a furnace grate; and the Sunday in summer we walked down the lane, talking about what to name our baby. I forgave myself for the years I spent angry at a contrived truth I'd invented because I needed to hold someone accountable for his death. After all, how do you not hear a train?

Ask the Great Plains. They will show you.

Bruce rests in the peace of the prairie ground, surrounded by the wind and the rocks and the never-ending vastness. The circle of our life together was small, but it was complete, and I realize now that he and I, too, are never-ending. No train could ever stop that.

A Time to Weep
Posted June 2000

In loving memory of Tony Fabri, who was killed in a car crash June 22, 2000.

The last time I saw Tony alive was the evening of June 20 when he stopped by our house to say hi. We sat on the porch and I don't remember what we talked about, but he looked good and smelled good and after his signature hug, his aftershave clung to me for hours. Tony's visits were always calming and familiar. I never imagined that was the last one.

Three nights later I sat on the porch getting acquainted with a new and unwelcome heartache, and I thought about duality and how our souls can know sadness and joy at the same time and how sometimes they are the same feeling. It's the only way I can explain the pain of losing him at the same time as the joy of knowing him.

Tony was to me a surrogate son, and to my daughters, a friend, confidant, and counselor. Unlike the seventeen-year-old male stereotype, Tony spoke in complete sentences, loved being with his family, and wasn't afraid to show emotion. He was stubborn and persistent and very persuasive.

Tony was a charmer.

He had a knack for making people feel special. If Tony thought someone was interesting, he didn't care how old they were, where they lived, or what they or their parents did for a living, he introduced himself and a friendship ensued.

I've seen many of his friends this week and they ask, "How can he be dead? We just talked to him. He was online. We were just out shopping together." I've heard some of them remember the times they and Tony had disagreed or weren't in the mood to see each other. Some wish they had contacted him one more time or told him more often how they felt about him.

To those of you who are feeling that way, remember: Tony and you were living your lives the way you always did, and your relationship survived the stubbornness and ignorance all friendships experience because the good times always transcended the bad. Tony knew how you felt about him because you know how Tony felt about you. Communication was rarely a problem for him.

But the elusive question, "Why?" still hangs in the air, damp and thick. The funeral is over, he's been laid to rest, and still I can't wrap my brain around this enormous truth. Tony's parents, Elliot and Debbie, and his sister, Lauren, and brother, Elliot, so stunned and confused, seemed to search everyone's eyes for the answers. And all we could do was say we're sorry, we don't know. I looked up to heaven that night on the porch and asked, "Where is God?" and Heaven replied, "Weeping, right beside all of you who grieve."

That's right, I thought. I forget that sometimes when the pain of grief, present and past, is so crushing. God is not sadistic or self-important. God doesn't pluck people out to serve him in heaven. The grace of God is strength and comfort and love and understanding when someone we love dies.

With life comes death, I understand that intellectually, but I don't believe in the finality of that explicit certainty. I know too well how death works, and the faith that comes from knowing an even greater truth — that with life comes more life — is the only thing that keeps me sane.

Tony's presence is too strong to be silenced by death. His ubiquitous spirit is alive in the songs he loved, the places he loved, and especially the people he loved. It is alive in the eyes of his mother and father, sister and brother.

Edward Hays, a priest, wrote a psalm as a voice for the dead, and in it he said: "Fear not nor grieve at my departure, you whom I have loved so much, for my roots and yours are forever intertwined." Peace, love and eternal connectedness: I believe these would be Tony's wishes for us. He will be present with us when we call on him. He will come to us to "open our blocked paths, to untangle our knots, and to be (our) avenue to God." As Cassie, my daughter, said, he's talking to us. We just have to know how to listen.

The world didn't stop June 22, but nothing will ever be the same again. I am humbled that God let me know Tony, that God let me call him my friend and surrogate son. How fortunate I am to have spent four years knowing he might show up at my house at any time. Debbie and Elliot's son was an incredible gift in life and will be a gift to us in death because we can spend the rest of our lives learning from him, from his love and generosity.

Tony, our dear son, brother, friend, keeper of all our memories, when you died, a piece of your family and friends went with you, and I hope these pieces of our lives bring you peace in paradise. You are a legend in our minds, the kind of man I want my sons to be. Your compassion pacified wounds deep and forgotten, your smile was the light that said "All is well." You made my daughters laugh and think deeply. You made them and so many others understand what it means to be a friend.

I think I speak for everyone who has ever known you when I say, "Thank you."

Grief 101
Posted May 2007

In a recent "My Turn" column in *Newsweek*, a woman wrote about her experience with a deacon who was officiating her father's funeral: "We were greeted by a grinning deacon who shook our hands and chirped, 'Isn't it a beautiful day? I'm so glad you have sun for your memorial!' I wanted to shake this woman. Couldn't she invoke a solemn tone for at least five seconds on the darkest morning of my life?"

What is it that makes people say and do things that are unwittingly hurtful to those who are grieving? My best guess is that grief isn't a feeling most people want to live with, feel, or witness daily, and yet grief springs from loss and loss can catch people like deer in the headlights.

It's not an easy thing to respond to someone who is grieving. Many people simply don't know what to say or do. Given my experiences with loss, this would be my list of what not to do or say.

1. Don't plan or ask about their future. I was dumbfounded by how many people said to me in the days following my husband's death, "Oh, you'll meet someone new," or "Do you think you'll get married again?"

I know they were trying to offer hope or to assure me, in awkward fashion, that life goes on. But when someone you love dies, you can't skip over the pain, no matter how difficult it is to feel, and as family and friends, we should not encourage it.

2. Don't ask for the deceased's personal belongings or (and you'd think this would be obvious) their children.

A) A day before the funeral, one of my sisters-in-law asked if her son could have my husband's archery equipment.

My reply: Blink…blink…blink.

B) On the day of the funeral, another sister-in-law said to another sister-in-law that she thought she should raise our daughter. That one still stings all these years later. I have no words except don't ever, ever ask that of a newly single parent. Babysit, yes. Raise? Absolutely not.

3. Don't avoid them. I was hurt when a few friends who lived nearby didn't come to the viewing or the funeral. Neither did they call or offer any kind of support.

I understand that I wasn't the only one who'd lost someone they loved. But if someone you care about has died, and you consider yourself a good friend, or if your family bond is tight, get over yourself and show up. Grief isn't a communicable disease, but it certainly should be communal.

4. Don't start or spread rumors. A few days after the funeral, someone started rumors that I was having an affair with the funeral director, and that I'd started drinking. Clearly they hadn't considered that, at the very least, I just had a baby and was nursing.

I know that rumors say more about the person who starts them and to those who spread them and that they are best left ignored, but when you've lost someone, your feelings are fragile. Untruths make the grief that much more difficult to bear. Don't assume anything about the person who is grieving and don't draw any conclusions about their actions until you talk to them.

5. Don't publish photos of the deceased's body. Death is big news in a small town and I knew there would most likely be mention of the accident in the papers. I was right, only I didn't expect there to be photos.

One was of Bruce's tractor ripped to shreds and the other's caption read: "The body of Bruce Bouwman can be seen in the center of the photograph alongside the tracks and covered with a tarp." Only, his body wasn't completely covered. His bootless feet protruded from the bottom, making the photo that much more sickening.

A newspaper's purpose is to inform the public, not sensationalize the death of an ordinary man; a farmer, father, husband, and friend who did nothing more than die unintentionally and in horrific fashion. Like those who spread rumors, an editor who publishes a photo like this does little more than serve themselves and not the public good.

6. Don't tell a person who is mourning that "time heals." Something my pastor said to me in the days after Bruce died has stayed with me, and I share it often with others who grieve. He said that time doesn't heal, it only gives us perspective.

At the moment he said that, I was angry.

"What do you mean time doesn't heal?" I cried. "It has to! It must! How else am I supposed to feel better and normal ever again if something doesn't heal me?"

"Time doesn't have the power to 'heal,'" he replied. "Healing implies it all goes away. But years from now, you'll be able to recall this time, and feel everything you feel at this very moment. In time, you will get stronger, you will feel joy again, you will build yourself up, but this comes from inside you, not because a certain amount of time passes.

"It's a lot of work and you won't be the same person you were before he died. You can't be."

In time, I understood that he was right, and once I accepted that grief is a journey down a long and arduous road, I no longer put a time line on when it "should" end because it doesn't.

Now for the "What to do" list. To support someone you care about who is grieving a loss:

1. Be there. Several of my friends and family members traveled hundreds of miles to be with me when Bruce died, not knowing what to expect when they got to my house. All they wanted was to be with me and offer their presence, and it was a huge comfort.

2. Listen, even in the silence. It's not easy knowing what to say. Silence can seem rude or uncomfortable, but let your loved one cry without you responding. Their tears are talking. You don't have to.

3. Offer a memory of the person who died. No one who grieves wants to forgot their loved one. They want to talk about them. Talking keeps them close. Sharing your stories lets them know that the person they loved was important to other people, too. If you were close to the person who died, this can be helpful in your own grief as well.

On what would have been our first wedding anniversary, Carlene was baptized. That afternoon, my friends and Bruce's friends came to our farm, many armed with grills, and we had a party. We ate and drank and told stories. We remembered, cried, and loved Bruce by doing exactly what he would have done if one of his friends had died.

Focusing on life, not death, is how best to process grief.

4. Write a note of care. If you can't be with your loved one in person, send a card, and I urge you to do more than sign your name. Always keep the person who is grieving in the forefront and don't make your message about you. If you don't know what to say, say that. Be honest. "I don't know what to say, but I'm thinking of you," relays more than you think it can. Even something as simple as "Love you" can suffice.

Don't be afraid to write the deceased's name. "I'm sorry _____ died." This is not inappropriate. Death is silence enough. Reading their name helps keep their life real and memory alive.

One of the nicest cards I received was from a woman I didn't know. She wrote a heartfelt letter about how sad she was for me. She was around my age, she had a baby, and her husband was a farmer. She wrote that while she obviously couldn't empathize with my situation, she could sympathize, and she sent me her warmest and kindest thoughts.

Even if you see and talk with the person who is grieving, writing a note or card offers you the opportunity to put into words what may have been difficult or inopportune to express in person.

5. Food is optional, but usually welcome. The person who is grieving the most might not feel like eating anything, but the people who visit probably will. Food is a universal language and can relay care and love in an abstract way.

6. Remember them. What often happens when someone dies is there is a flurry of attention paid to the person or people closest to the deceased, and then…crickets. We go home after the funeral and back to our normal lives, while those who are grieving are learning to live without a central figure from their lives. I'm not suggesting you call every day, unless you feel that would be helpful. Check in with an email or a card letting them know you're thinking of them and are available if they need anything.

Invite them to coffee or to have a meal and don't be offended if they say no. Keep trying. If your friend or loved one isn't comfortable socializing, offer to bring over takeout.

Grieving is difficult, and it's not easy, as people who support those who've suffered a loss, to know what to do or say. If you find yourself at a loss, put yourself in their shoes. What would you want to hear? What would you want people to do? What do you think would be most helpful?

Don't be like the deacon in the "My Turn" column, offering joy in the midst of others' sorrow. Our job is not to look on the bright side or to "solve" our loved one's grief. Be there, be honest, listen, offer kind, supportive words, and most important, remember them. In doing that, you're not only helping those who grieve, you honor the person who died.

Courtney Love
Posted May 2007

I have a friend who is friends with a woman who last month met Courtney Love by chance in Hawaii. The two of them spent an evening in a hotel bar smoking cigarettes and talking.

Nothing cool like that ever happens to me, and even if it did, you wouldn't think I'd have enough in common with Courtney Love to keep her attention for longer than it would take for me to light a match for her cigarette. I don't smoke or do drugs, although I can swear like a sailor. I was never in rehab. I respect authority, for the most part, and don't wear a lot of lipstick. I also don't wear cool clothes and I can't play the guitar or write music. I'm certainly not an actress and I was never married to a rock star.

Yes, it would seem that Courtney Love and I are quite opposite. However, she recently decided to sell Kurt Cobain's personal belongings and it made me think maybe we're not so different after all. Both of us were widowed soon after giving birth and likewise, I had to make decisions about my husband's personal belongings. That could be a subject we could chat about over a few martinis, maybe.

When someone dies, especially unexpectedly, they leave behind all the ordinary living kinds of things—a toothbrush and razor, combs, aftershave, clothes, letters from old lover's, tax records, photos, school yearbooks, newspaper clippings, vacation journals, maybe a car and all the crap stuffed under the seats, trinkets and gifts that decorate the house, a CD or record collection, movies, a bike, a favorite blanket…the list goes on and on.

Think about it. If you died today, all the stuff you own and use that make your life the way it is would become someone else's to deal with, and all that stuff has to go somewhere.

"My house is like a mausoleum," Love told Spinner.com. "My daughter doesn't need to inherit a giant bag full of flannel shirts…A sweater, a guitar, and the lyrics to '(Smells Like) Teen Spirit'—that's what my daughter gets. And the rest of it we'll just…sell."

Except for his bowling shirt, I gave away Bruce's clothes when he died, and I threw out his toiletries. But I've hauled around boxes of his stuff from house to house to house, from marriage to marriage to marriage, and I'm thinking it's time to lighten the load a little. Maybe it's time to let our daughter decide what she wants to keep and what she wants to sell or toss. I have our wedding album, his letters, and a memory. That's all I need.

Well, that and perhaps the television.

Recently, I gave away all the things I was going to sell at a garage sale because I don't have the time to host a garage sale. One of the things in my garage (and in every garage I've had since 1983) is a Hitachi turn-dial thirteen-inch television my parents gave Bruce and me for our wedding. When the guys were loading the truck yesterday to haul all my stuff away, the television was on the chopping block. I thought I was ready to let it go. But when I saw it there on the floor, waiting its turn to be lugged away like all the other stuff, I caved and told them to leave it.

I couldn't let it go, even though it's just sitting there reminding me of what was. I don't need it, I don't use it, so why do I keep it around?

I think it's because a TV is more tangible than a photograph. Bruce touched it, watched it, moved the antennae around on it, even rapped it a few times to get a better signal. With my head on his lap, we watched the final episode of *M*A*S*H* on that television, as well as *Shogun*, *Winds of War*, *East of Eden* (the movie that inspired us to name our baby Caleb if it was a boy), *Family Ties*, *Fridays*, and *Saturday Night Live*. We fell asleep watching *The Adventures of Rocky and Bullwinkle* cartoons the first few days of Carlene's life with her tucked between us.

With no remote, we had to get up and change the channel. I especially liked to watch him walk to the TV and bend over to turn the knob.

The TV is the one functional thing I kept from our life and I don't want to let that go. Not yet, at least.

Maybe one day I'll run into Courtney Love and we can drink and talk about the merits of keeping an old television set. I'm pretty sure she'd understand.

About Last Night
Posted October 2014

There have been moments in my life when I've sensed Bruce's presence. While warm and bittersweet, I understand those feelings to be resurrected memories of the connection we had when he was alive; me subconsciously sating some need I hadn't completely identified. I don't believe those vague presences stem from a visit by his spirit.

That's why I can't explain what happened last night.

I often employ the "Just ignore it, it will go away" approach to healthcare. But after a months-long battle with hip pain, in which the last few days I've been barely able to walk, I finally mentioned it to my doctor. She ordered x-rays and as I wait for the results, I'm living with limited mobility and a crap-ton of pain which makes me feel trapped, angry, alone, and scared, bordering on the edge of self-pity. And I hate self-pity, especially in the middle of the night.

My boyfriend Jim and I were at my house last night, and he fell asleep as soon as his head hit the pillow. My bed tends to envelop us like a taco and I knew my hip would not be comfortable within such limited space, so I got up and limped to the spare room where I lay awake, playing Canasta on my phone.

After a few hours, I found a comfortable position on my side facing the wall. Hugging the top of a body pillow I'd tucked between my legs, I started to fall asleep, but not before Jim walked in the room and, saying nothing, placed a hand on my shoulder and one on the back of my neck and kissed my head, just above my ear. I felt safe and loved, and more than that, I wasn't afraid anymore.

I woke up at 4 a.m. when again, Jim came in the room.

"Why aren't you in bed?" he whispered. He sat down on the edge of the bed and stroked my hair.

"I couldn't get comfortable and I didn't want to wake you," I said softly.

"You can wake me up anytime."

"I know. But you knew where I was. You came in around 1:00, remember? You kissed my head."

"This is the first time I've been up," he said. "I didn't know you weren't in bed until just now."

"What do you mean?" I started to cry. "But I felt so safe. I was finally able to sleep. I thought it was you."

"No, it wasn't me." He moved his hand to my leg, covered in three layers of blankets, and began to rub the top of my hip. "But someone wanted you to know they cared."

When I'd crawled into that spare bed, it didn't occur to me to reach out to anyone, dead or alive. I was entirely alone, physically and mentally. I made no effort to meditate or pray. I was resigned to my fear, and I imagined every scenario I could think of for how, or if, I would walk normally again. I assure you, I was in the throes of self-pity. My mind was all about me. I had no conscious thought to partner with Bruce or a deity or anything else to help me through.

Whoever or whatever touched my shoulder and kissed my head knew better than me what I needed and gave me the one thing I could not give myself: peace. Even skeptical me knows not to attempt to explain, justify, or otherwise dispute such a gift.

Grief Really Shouldn't End
Posted August 2018

Recently, the husband of a dear friend was killed when a tree limb fell on him while he was working in his yard. A freak and random accident, it has left my friend stunned and so very, very sad.

I've written many times about grief and how it bounces in and out and around our lives and lands sometimes in the most unexpected places at the most inopportune times (like there's ever a good time for loss). But you know grief. It doesn't wait for an appointment.

Sudden loss can feel like an ambush. It barges in and takes over everything, and the accompanying emotions stun us, infiltrate and define our most tender feelings, and they never really leave, even when we don't feel them as acutely anymore.

Time goes by and we go about our lives, not thinking about grief, perhaps even (foolishly) thinking we've conquered it, feeling like we're so over _____ (fill in your loss), and then WHAM! We find ourselves in a friend's kitchen, helplessly hugging her as she cries desperately in her own mourning, grieving a loss that, while uniquely hers, feels very familiar. The emotions from our own day of loss flood back, perhaps not as strong, but it is grief's way of reminding us that it never, ever goes away.

There are times, too, when grief is more subtle and refuses to readily identify itself. Your life, by all accounts, is fine. You're holding it together, and you even dared to be happy and smile again. Then, seemingly out of nowhere, you wake up one morning with an overwhelming sense of dread and sadness, feeling like you can't pull the blanket off from around your head. You wander around dazed for a while—a day, a week, a month, longer—unable to put your finger on the culprit because, you know, that death/loss was so long ago and you're, like, totally over it, so it must be something else.

But it's not.

I write this to remind us that grief is not something we ever finish. And honestly, I don't think it's supposed to end.

I'm not saying we should feel miserable all the time or constantly remind ourselves of what we've lost. But loss and grief are inevitable for each one of us. Instead of trying to drink it away, drug it away, fuck it away, eat it away, or work it away, why not use the hell out of it and grow empathy where perhaps there wasn't any? Even if someone's loss isn't exactly the same as ours, understanding that the experience of loss is overarching and universal can train us to be more understanding, kind, helpful, and, when warranted, involved in bringing change to what is wrong.

Grief can strengthen us and, sadly, destroy us, but there's no in between. The thing is, though, that even when we think it's destroying us, it just might be strengthening us, teaching us more about ourselves than we ever wanted to know. This is not to say that what brought us to grieve is somehow a good thing. Personally, I'd rather my (and my friend's) husband was alive, or the baby I miscarried had been born, or that the things I lost in the fire hadn't burned, or that my brother's memory was intact, or that any of the other losses I've experienced in my life hadn't happened. But all of these losses make up my real life. Subsequently, grief, too, is a part of my real life, and I want grief to have meaning and a purpose, even if that purpose is simply to listen to a friend who is hurting.

P.S. We witnessed a simple and bittersweet lesson in grief recently when a female orca whale carried her dead baby on her back for seventeen days before finally letting it go. She didn't adhere to some cultural agenda that said you get a few days to grieve and then you're supposed to get on with your life. She grieved in her own way, and so should we.

Firsts
November 2019

Last weekend, two of my four grandkids came to stay for a few nights — the oldest, Claire, who is twelve, and the youngest, Audrey, who is six. I live in a small house with only a twin-sized bed in my office and an air mattress for visitors. With floor space at a premium, where I drop the air mattress is decided with careful calculation.

Audrey prefers the air mattress because it's easier for my dog Zuzu (whose name you have to say in a very high pitch to capture the vocal rendition of Audrey saying her name, almost like an angel is singing it) to jump in bed with her. But for this combination of grandchildren, I decided it would be best if Claire slept on the air mattress in the living room and Audrey slept in the spare bed. That way they'd have room for their bags and a place to change their clothes in the office without the acrobatics of maneuvering around a mattress in the middle of an already small room.

"Nooooooooooo!" said Audrey when I told her my plan. "I want to sleep on the air mattress!"

"The air mattress will be in the living room. Do you want to sleep in the living room?"

"Nooooooooooo!"

"Then you'll sleep in the spare bed."

"Nooooooooooo!"

This went on for five minutes until Claire and I were able to reassure her that Zuzu could, in fact, jump up on the spare bed and would probably happily do so more than once in the middle of the night.

The rest of the weekend was mostly resistance-free. Jim and the girls worked on wood projects in the garage. Claire shot the BB gun. We played Skip-Bo, ate mussels (even Audrey, the pickiest eater ever), went to see the downtown Christmas tree in the rain, and watched *Home Alone*. Claire also mentioned her late grandmother Julia intermittently throughout the weekend, in that spontaneous, unconscious way we honor those who have died by recalling the ordinary, everyday things we loved about them. "I remember when Grandma would..." or "Grandma used to say..." and Claire laughed as she talked, because Grandma Julia always made her laugh.

Julia died in February after a years-long battle with cancer. It's been a difficult year of firsts for our grandchildren and the rest of the family, and now here we are at the front door of perhaps the most difficult of firsts: the holidays.

As is the tradition of many families on Thanksgiving, we go around the table and say one thing we're grateful for. Mine this year is Julia.

Shortly after her death, I wrote about the last time I saw Julia, but I was too close to the loss to write much. I had to let the grief be there and not try to explain it to myself or anyone else. I needed to simply miss her and to honor the gaping hole in my heart by doing nothing other than feel the wind pass through it. Now, though the tears still come, the sharpness of her death has softened somewhat. With nine months of perspective, I remember more than I would have in the tight confines of grief and I'm better able to offer a sincere thank you to the powers that be that gave us Julia, where in March, I was angry.

Obviously, without Julia there would be no Matt (my son-in-law) and therefore no Claire, Luca, Mae, or Audrey. But what I'm most grateful for is how she lived her life as a grandmother and friend and even as a woman dying. When I saw her the last time, I held her hand and thanked her for showing me how to be the grandma who keeps a stash of color books and crayons in her car, snacks and wet wipes in her purse, and says yes to drive-through French fries. She looked at me a little confused and said, "Oh, honey, you would have figured it out!" Nope, no I wouldn't have. Not in that Julia way anyway.

When Claire was born, my heart was full of so many strong emotions that it took me a few weeks to parse out and understand them all. I was afraid I wouldn't be able to share her with others. Then when I saw Julia holding Claire and gushing all those same emotions over her, I knew that was the kind of love I wished for my granddaughter, the kind all of us can never have enough of.

There are times when I feel a burden of being Claire, Luca, Mae, and Audrey's only living grandmother. Then I ask myself what would Julia do if I was the grandmother who died and I know for sure that what he wanted to see and I couldn't change that. In the end, I needed an emotional connection he wasn't able to give, and by the time I learned I was pregnant, we were no longer seeing each other.

He reluctantly, yet with a sense of obligation, relinquished his parental rights, although I brought Cassie to see him a few times when she was a baby. When she was five, I was remarried and we moved out of state. He got married and had three sons, although he promised his wife he wouldn't tell them about their sister. I continued to send him photos of her every year, and a few times when I visited Minnesota, we would meet for coffee and I would catch him up on her life. One year he gave me a Pooky plush toy (Garfield the Cat's teddy bear) and asked me to give it to her. I wasn't a big Garfield fan, but he and Cassie were. Her taste in humor, in this case, was nature, not nurture.

Lee re-met Cassie when she was sixteen. We agreed to meet at his office, and we spent an hour of uncomfortable moments of him telling Cassie it was my fault he didn't get to know her, and that he loved her and he loved me and that he always did, like he thought somehow Cassie could heal his heart, if only she could get me to listen to him. We left, exhausted, and his future communications with Cassie were sporadic, and with me, even fewer.

One of the last times I "talked" to Lee was in 2015 when I sent him a text message as I decorated my Christmas tree on Cassie's birthday, December 12. I was listening to the Moody Blues' album *December*. The song "A Winter's Tale" reminded me of our relationship, at least from my perspective, and I shared it with him.

> *It's a love that could never be*
> *Though it meant a lot to you and me*
> *On a world-wide scale, we're just another winter's tale*

He wrote back saying he still wished things had been different. I couldn't share his wish, as I was the one who let us go thirty years earlier and even now wouldn't change my decision, but I thanked him, as I always did, for our daughter, and told him that I couldn't imagine life without her. He said neither could he.

Lee finally told his sons about Cassie, because you know secrets, the big ones don't stay secret forever. Cassie met them a few years ago, and their love for each other is as genuine as if they'd known each other from the days they were born. Lee seemed happy to have them all together in his house, even though he expressed that happiness in his passive-aggressive, detached way.

Lee died on April 24, 2020, alone in a nursing home, but thankfully in his sleep. He hadn't remembered anyone or anything for several months. He took with him secrets no one could unearth and emotions he couldn't share. But I know for certain that he loved his daughter, his sons, and me in his own enigmatic way that we will never fully understand. May he finally find that peace that was stolen from him years ago, and rest knowing that we loved him, too.

3. Parenting

"A person's life is not a series of dramatic events for which he or she is applauded or exiled, but a slow accumulation of days, seasons, years, fleshed out by the generational weight of one's family and anchored by a land-bound sense of place."

—From *The Solace of Open Spaces* by Gretel Ehrlich

When I started writing my newspaper column in 1998, I hesitated to write about my children. I wasn't comfortable inviting the world, or at least our little town, into their lives. But as my writing voice emerged, it became clear that my niche was telling stories, both mine and others', for the purpose of starting a conversation with a reading community. I realized that my family and that "land-bound sense of place" shaped my world view and, therefore, what and how I wrote. Excluding my children from my columns felt like I was writing from only half of who I was, so I made an agreement with my daughters and stepsons that I wouldn't publish anything embarrassing or private, and if I had any reservation about something I'd written about them, I would talk to them about it before it went in the paper.

We may not all be parents, but we were all children once, and the universal experience of childhood—good, bad, or somewhere in between—was fertile ground for the kind of dialogue and reflection I always hoped my writing would affect.

Sixteen-Year-Old Life Changer
Posted March 1999

Well, here you are, sixteen years old today and I can't think of what to buy you to mark this crossroads birthday. What do I get a girl who has changed my life so profoundly, expected nothing less than everything from me, and taught me that promises are not contingencies?

I thank God every day for you, that you came into my life when you did. After your dad died, you were my only reason to live. Our middle-of-the-night feedings, watching cartoons, the dozens of car trips that first year to visit your grandparents and singing "Apples and Bananas" and "Jelly Man Kelly" over and over to pass the time, waking to find you peeking out at me between the bars on your crib and playing peek-a-boo when I should have been getting ready for work—these were not just distractions from sadness. While undergirded by loss, our life together has always been tightly bound by love and wonder.

I was overwhelmed by how protective my love could be the day you came home from first grade and cried, which you rarely did, because the other girls in your class wouldn't invite you to play with them during recess. It broke my heart to think no one would give you a chance—you, the most quiet and sweet girl I've ever known. It's why today I would defend you against anyone who hurts you.

I know you don't always understand the animosity I harbor for people who have caused you pain, especially the ones you have forgiven. Maybe someday when your daughter cries because someone pushed her down, called her a name, broke her heart or a promise, you'll understand.

From the day you colored your walls red and told me you didn't know who did it to the day you walked out the door with a boy on your arm and high heels on your feet and you gave me a little wave from his car, I've watched in awe as you've grown up with the kind of conscientiousness and self-awareness some people never have if they live to be one hundred.

As each year passes, you peel back the secrets of life—the freedom that comes from tying your own shoes and staying out past dark, and the knowledge that it's OK to make mistakes and to eat leftovers for breakfast.

Soon I will teach you to drive, which will be a far different experience than when I taught you to ride your bike. I ran behind you while you rode, white-knuckled, on your two-wheeler, my hand only resting on the back of the seat. It made you think I was in control. You didn't know you were doing all the work. You didn't want me to let go, yet you wanted me to let go. You saw ahead of you, with the wind blowing across your face, the freedom you wanted and feared. The decision was yours, and after days of practice, you yelled "Let go!" and you sped up as I slowed down.

Now it's me who sits at the junction of your emancipation and my desire to hang on to the familiar. I want to let go but I want to hang on, steady you with my guiding hand, make decisions for you. But as you've told me many times lately, you can think for yourself and you hate it when people treat you as though you can't or don't.

I promise I'll try to never be one of those people.

I hope God lets your dad take a look at you every once in a while, during those times you're singing or long-jumping or sleeping between your flannel sheets with the yellow blanket we wrapped you in when we took you home from the hospital.

It's the least God could do for the man who was the first to hold you, sing to you, and rock you to sleep.

Happy birthday, honey. No gift I give you could show you how grateful I am that you are my daughter. The true gift is that without you these past sixteen years, I would never have learned the meaning of unconditional love.

Staying One Step Ahead of the Second Child
Posted November 1999

Next year at this time, my youngest daughter will almost be sixteen. She figured this out the other day while I was driving her to work or cheerleading practice or a football game or maybe Walmart. I can't remember. I just drive.

"Isn't that exciting!" she said. "Then I can drive myself everywhere!"

She was born twenty months after her sister, and ever since she's been playing catch-up, always wanting to be her sister's age.

When she was eight she wanted to be ten. At eleven, she was convinced her life would begin at thirteen. Now, at fourteen, the magic age is sixteen—the age to drive, date, and plan her life for when she's eighteen.

I can understand her feeling that she has an inherent right to the same timetable as her sister. When they were small children, I lumped them together as a group rather than seeing them as individuals of differing ages.

Youngest Daughter stopped taking naps and gave up Barbies the same time as Oldest Daughter, and started listening to (and stopped listening to) New Kids on the Block when her sister did.

But age became an issue when it was time for the big stuff, like staying up a half-hour later, putting on fingernail polish by herself, riding in the front seat, shaving her legs, wearing makeup, getting her ears pierced a second time, and dating. She had to wait.

"Wait?" she exclaims each time her sister gets a new privilege. "That's not fair!"

"Those are the rules."

"Well, when can I?"

"When you are your sister's age."

"Do you promise?"

"Yes," I always sigh. "I promise."

Parents, learn this lesson well: Never promise a child anything hoping she will forget. She won't. And if you do promise something, make sure you write it down. Verbatim. Have it notarized. Sign it in blood. Or you'll be matching wits and memories with a kid who has documented proof you made a promise exactly as you said it years before while you were making Thanksgiving dinner for thirty and would say anything to get her out of the kitchen.

This lesson applies mostly to the second child. With a first child, parents are fledglings and rarely promise anything because they have no idea what they're doing. For example, if your oldest child asks to stay up a half-hour later, you might say something like, "I'll think about it," and then run to the bookshelf for advice as soon as she's out of the room.

I'm going to let you in on a secret the books never tell: When you render your decision about the first child's request, your second child is taking it all in, memorizing the date, the time, the exact age of the first child (to the day) and the place you were standing when you said, "Yes, you may stay up a half-hour later tonight."

Be prepared when your second child comes to you, detailed charts and analysis in hand, at exactly the same time in her life and asks to stay up a half-hour later. If you have forgotten when you allowed the first child the same privilege, you will have no defense. God help you if you say no.

If these second-born children could apply these awesome

memorization and organizational skills to their education, they'd all be rocket scientists, brain surgeons, or concert pianists. However, being adamant about being right is usually reserved only for fairness (as they perceive it) in family matters. Being driven to memorize their spelling words or the periodic table is not in the same league as showing up their mother or older sister.

Being second doesn't always mean having to wait, or being vigilant for injustices or wearing hand-me-downs, though. It does have its advantages. My youngest makes mental notes every time her sister and I have a difference of opinion and some kind of punishment is handed down. With this advanced knowledge, the youngest rarely repeats the mistakes of her sister. Where she doesn't avoid punishment (or at least a dirty look) is when she reminds me of my mistakes.

The second child is almost always compared to the older child, especially if they're the same gender. But second children rarely walk the path tread by their older sibling. My oldest is a bit reserved, a little shy. It is my youngest who makes the most noise in our world, the one who will not be ignored, the one who will try the things her sister won't. She is the child my mother couldn't wait for me to have—the one who is just like me.

And I wouldn't have her any other way. Her smile lights up a room. She can tune into a person's emotional frequency just by looking at their face. She'll be anything she wants to someday because she is brave and honest and can look the truth in the eye and not run away.

Yeah, so she wants to be older. Who, at fourteen, didn't? If the years have taught me anything, it's that our desire to be older than we are stops at about twenty-five, the age auto insurance rates (and some body parts) start to drop.

Besides, when she's twenty-five, I'll be forty-five wishing I was thirty-five. Thank God for my grandmother who used to tell me that one day, we'll all be happy to be any age.

Common Ground

Little Women Meet Ren and Stimpy
Posted December 1999

If the number of stepfamilies continues to increase in the twenty-first century, as they are expected to, then we need better press. Most are not like Cinderella's messed up family.

I never expected to be a stepmother, but I am, and life, for the most part, is normal, as normal as it can be when a woman raising two teenage girls meets and marries a man with two young boys.

This coming together of our families is a little like Little Women meet Ren and Stimpy. My girls have learned to accept, or at least ignore, the boys' burping contests, and the boys pass off the girls singing Dave Matthews Band songs loudly in the basement or prepping in front of a mirror as just weird.

Bras don't dry over chairs in the kitchen anymore, and the froufrou lady stuff shares space in the bathroom with bubblegum flavored toothpaste and Star Wars toothbrushes. Marbles are strewn throughout the living room, and plastic bloody eyeballs are sometimes hidden in the refrigerator.

The boys taught the girls their favorite song: "Beans, beans, they're good for your heart. The more you eat the more you..." You can guess the rest. The girls have turned the boys on to "cool" music—no more Raffi in this house.

The girls read *Chicken Soup* books and Brontë novels. The boys prefer *Captain Underpants*. The boys tell a lot of stories, usually the "Know what?" variety, and they take every opportunity to say the word "butt." In their world, having smelly feet is a good thing. So is pro wrestling and Pokémon.

Unlike Cinderella's stepmother, the chores I make them do are pretty benign. They clear the dinner table, dry dishes, and put the toilet lid down when they're done. I'm kidding about the toilet lid. They never remember to do that.

They like to talk about their futures as astronaut paleontologists or anthropologist brain surgeons. We're especially encouraging Andy's most recent dream: to be a guitarist *and* a professional baseball player — professions that are sure to keep his dad and me comfortable in our retirement.

We're fairly sure Kevin will be a detective or a biologist. He likes to crawl in bed with us and explain how ladybugs eat aphids, and he spies on the girls while they are watching television using his telescope. He also checks the cats for fingerprints.

This quasi Brady Bunch life didn't just happen. Adjusting to each other's personalities, needs, fears, and aversions was often difficult. But of all the relationships in this new family, the stepmother-stepson one was the hardest to forge.

By the time I married their father last year, the boys and I had interacted on several occasions, few of which were particularly memorable. Their behavior usually translated into: Who is this strange woman with our dad, and why should we listen to her?

I did few things right in their eyes and spent many frustrated moments in tears asking friends what I was doing wrong.

Finding my place in their lives and they in mine took time. But with each visit, we saw how important we were to their father, and realized, subconsciously of course, that if we wanted a part of him, we had to accept a part of each other as well.

I think our difficulty was mostly due to my desire to nurture them as I nurtured my own children, and their fear of allowing me to nurture them. Since they already had a mother, they didn't feel they could be true to her while letting me wipe away their tears or laugh at their jokes. The words, "You're not my mom!" frequently rolled off their tongues, especially if I didn't allow them to jump on the couch or swing from their bunkbeds. There were times I wanted to give up.

But the tears, the time, the patience, and the prayers gradually paid off. I'm not exactly sure when or how it all happened, but their most recent visit demonstrated how far we've come in three years.

Andy, who just turned eight, doesn't usually want to be hugged. The other night, he had a bad dream. He started crying because he missed his mom, but he let me hold him and stroke his hair and tell him it was OK to be sad. He thanked me the next day for listening to him. I told him I listened because I loved him. He said he loved me, too. I'll bet Cinderella never said those words to her stepmother.

Kevin, on the other hand, is still a little boy of six, and likes to be sung to and to sleep with his stuffed dog, "Pup." He won't let any of us catch him under the mistletoe, but he and Pup always snuggle on the couch with me while we watch holiday movies. He listens to me when I correct him, holds my hand when we cross the street, and climbs on my lap while we play a game on the computer—oblivious acts now that three years ago would have been met with resistance.

Being a stepmother isn't about being cruel and nasty, and warts are optional. It's a lot like mothering, a little like friendship, and a lot like love. In fact, it's a pretty good deal. I inherited two terrific boys without going through labor, highchairs, or potty training.

It's a great beginning to happily ever after.

Thoughts on a Belly-Button Piercing
Posted November 2000

After she had her ears pierced the second time, I told my youngest daughter she wasn't allowed any more piercings until she was sixteen.

Guess how old she'll be in a few weeks?

And do you suppose she forgot what I said ten years ago?

Not a chance, though I really thought she'd choose a body part above the neck.

When Cassie was four years old, she insisted she was a big girl and, like her older sister, she wanted to get her ears pierced. I said OK, and afterwards, Cassie was really good about cleaning her ear lobes and twirling the studs often to help them heal. After six weeks, when it was time to take out the studs and put in regular earrings, she cried as I removed the studs. We let the holes close.

When she was six, Cassie promised, promised, promised she would let me take out the studs and put in real earrings if I let her get her ears pierced again. God help me, but I believed her. This time, when the six weeks were up, she didn't cry, and she's been wearing earrings ever since.

I asked her why, since she remembered the first time she had her ears pierced, she wanted her belly button pierced.

"It'll look cool," she said.

Fair enough. At least I didn't have to pay for it. That was our agreement.

Here's something I didn't need to know: my daughter has the kind of belly button that body piercers love. But when you're holding your daughter's hand as she lay on an old doctor's table and a man in latex gloves holding a clamp and needle is hovering over her stomach, you have to talk about something.

Sitting in the waiting area before the piercing, I was the only parent in the room with their child, and for a moment, I thought maybe it would have been better if Cassie had done this behind my back. After all, what kind of mom signs a consent form allowing some stranger to stick a needle through her baby's belly button?

There were three other girls in the waiting room. One was pregnant, one said her baby was at home with a sitter, and one held hands with her boyfriend. The girl who'd recently given birth was chain-smoking in the corner. She was going to get her tongue pierced, and she was noticeably shaking. She said she wasn't eighteen yet, but that she had papers proving she was an emancipated minor. If anyone needed a mom at that moment, I think it was her.

There was a tobacco shop next to the waiting room, and I wandered over there while we waited for the body piercer to arrive. I used to buy albums at a place like it in Minneapolis called the Electric Fetus. They sold music up front, and in the back, they sold pipes, roach clips, papers, screens, and rollers. I've never understood why, since pot was illegal, you could buy paraphernalia. Maybe I'm wrong, but I don't think people smoke North Carolina-grown tobacco from a bong.

After my trip down memory lane, I went back to the waiting room and sat next to Cassie. It was a strange juxtaposition of people. Cassie's boyfriend, a high school football player, had joined us and was watching a football game on the TV in the corner. The emancipated minor was still smoking; the pregnant girl was twirling her tongue ring; the other girl and her boyfriend stared—deadpan—at the tattooing equipment. I tapped my foot while Cassie sighed.

Finally, the body piercer arrived, and thank God, he looked normal.

What I expected was a large hairy man wearing a denim shirt with the sleeves ripped off, fringe hanging down past massive biceps tattooed with snakes and dancing girls. I expected a deep gravelly voice, a wallet attached to a chain, cowboy boots, and no personality. The kind of guy you'd see in an Ozzy video. The kind of guy you'd call Sir.

But this body piercer had only a few piercings that I could see. He had short hair, a cell phone, and said he was an aspiring phlebotomist. He explained the procedure and the aftercare, and he answered Cassie's quintessential question: would it hurt? There's no blood, he said, and just a little pain.

As he cleaned her belly button area and talked about what great belly button skin she had, I thought about how much trouble her belly button gave me when she was a newborn. The moment was too weird to think of anything else.

Babies don't come with an instruction booklet, so for those who don't know, they go home from the hospital with a stub of umbilical cord attached. I'd taken a baby home from the hospital before so I knew the drill. Clean it with a cotton swab and betadine and keep it outside the diaper. My oldest daughter's belly button stump fell off like a champ a few weeks after she was born, but Cassie's...ugh. Her little stump got infected and I thought for sure it was going to kill her.

Now here she was piercing the damn thing.

It's been a few days now. Her skin is healing well. Cassie seems to be having better luck with her belly button than I did. The only problem she's having is with me. I keep forgetting I can't give her the Pillsbury Doughboy treatment for a while.

Blackbird Fly
Posted May 2001

"Blackbird singing in the dead of night, take these broken wings and learn to fly. All your life, you were only waiting for this moment to arise."

—Lennon & McCartney

You asked me, "What do you want, Mom? What do you think I should do?" And it was clear by your tone of voice that you expected me to say something customary like, "I just want you to be happy," but with a choked-up, guilt-ridden undertone that said "...but keep in mind I'd be happy if you stayed here."

Weren't you surprised when I didn't?

I don't have eyes in the back of my head for nothing, my daughter. Yes, I want you to be happy, but I've learned a thing or two about you in these eighteen years, and I know the life you've secretly dreamed about for years will die if you don't leave this town and see for yourself what lies beyond these hills.

You have an adventurous spirit and a cautious heart. The combination has served you well so far and you must trust it won't let you down in the future. You've learned there is no monster under the bed, no boogey man in the closet, no sandman, and no such thing as ghosts, yet you know there are bigger mysteries to solve and other truths to uncover out there somewhere all on your own. To not live where your heart and head can be free or to deny yourself that place of self-discovery would be placing yourself on a certain and predictable course, and God knows after years of listening to me tell you what the world is like, you're entitled to discover it for yourself.

So...what do I want? That's a question I've been thinking about and trying to answer since you were born. This is what I've come up with so far:

I want you to be happy in your own skin, to be at peace with your decisions, and to visit the Rocky Mountains in the winter.

I want you to drink good wine and see the midnight sun and walk along the Champs-Elysées with your best friend.

I want you to have babies when you're ready, and visit your grandparents once a year. I want you to never forget your sister's and stepbrothers' birthdays, and to go to Jasper once in a while and place flowers on your dad's grave.

I want you to never know an overdue bill, an IRS audit, or a broken tailpipe you can't afford to fix. I want you to concentrate on what you do that makes you successful and to not dwell on failures.

I want you to come home from wherever you are when you're homesick and to go back again feeling stronger for having been home, because I'll always be here for you, and you can wash your clothes while I make you manicotti and chocolate cake. Your room will still be purple, and I won't rent it out or turn it into the hot tub room like I threatened.

You see, I don't care where you go to college as long as you get the education you need to be what you want to be.

I don't care where you lay your head at night as long as it's warm and safe and, when it's right, with the person who loves you more than life.

I don't care what you do for a living as long as it doesn't hurt other people, that it envelops your God-given talents and gifts, and that it gives you satisfaction and affords you the kind of home you can relax in at the end of the day.

I trust you. I have faith in you. But mostly I love you, and love is the reason I can let go. I'm going to hurt for a while, and I'll probably cry all the way home after helping you move into your dorm. But I don't want you to feel you've caused me pain. Love is just like that sometimes.

I'll miss the smell of your perfume floating up the stairs after you leave for school. I'll miss hearing you tell me good night and feeling your kiss on my cheek before you go to bed. I'll miss seeing your face every day, our spontaneous talks in the kitchen, and the way you play with the dogs.

But while I'll miss you very much, I know I'll still be your mother when you're frustrated, your mom when you need advice, and your mommy when you need money or a hug.

Your moment is here, my girl, and you're ready to fly. And that is truly what I think you should do.

Common Ground

Signing Papers
Posted December 2001

I'm being weaned from my children by my children. At seventeen and eighteen, Cassie and Carlene don't need me for many things anymore, except maybe to buy face wash, body lotion, or tampons. Then it's not really me they need, but my Visa card.

From the minute they were born, I've been letting go. I let them go with the nurses to be cleaned, weighed, and measured. I let them get on a bus to go to their first day of kindergarten. I let them go to birthday parties, sleep-overs, field trips, and to the mall and movies with their friends. I've even let them go on dates with boys I didn't like, not because I trusted the boys, but because I trusted my girls. And trust is at the heart of letting go.

While Carlene grew up, her letting go of me was harder than me letting go of her. She hated day care, she wanted her first-grade teacher to call me after a thunderstorm one afternoon, and she usually sat on my lap when strangers or people she hadn't seen in a while were in the room. As she got older, though, Carlene grew a strong backbone, and combined with her level-headedness, she's turned into a strong young woman, even though I still buy her razors and shampoo.

On the opposite end of parenting is Cassie. Our letting go experiences have been of her pushing me rather than me pushing her. She had no problem disappearing into clothes racks when she was two years old while we were out shopping, leaving me frantically looking for her. She couldn't wait to go to school and loved it when I hired a babysitter if I went out. I always knew she needed me in some esoteric way, but she hasn't given up the secret of why.

She's done some fast talking and gentle pushing lately to help me face the hardest letting go of her yet. Last Tuesday, I signed a consent form allowing Cassie to join the Army Reserve. She made this decision before September 11, and I was mostly OK with it since she could finish high school without interruption, and go to college while doing her military work. Then as I watched the World Trade Center buildings collapse and saw the Pentagon on fire and the smoldering airplane debris in a field not far south from where we lived, I decided there was no way in hell I was going to let her join anything that might put her in the middle of whatever was coming.

But when she came home from school that day, she was more determined than ever to sign up.

I knew out of my fear I could be the control freak I'm known to be and refuse to let her join, to make her wait until she was eighteen and no longer needed my permission. But I've spent seventeen years reigning in this child and to hold her back might break her.

After all, this is a girl who, when she was three, thought she could stick a penny in an outlet like it was a vending machine. When the lights flickered, I heard a "snap" and felt a bump on the floor. I ran in to her room and there she was, blinking and stunned, and a penny, bent and burned, lay near the outlet. I didn't punish her. I figured the electric shock was lesson enough.

This is the same girl who, when she was seven, decided to visit her eighty-year-old friend for five hours without telling me where she was. How do you get mad at someone who's doing a good thing, but who didn't follow the rules?

Just as control defined me as a parent, dichotomy defined Cass.

I read the consent form. It was perfectly clear. My signature meant I understood Cassie might be put in dangerous, life-threatening situations should her reserve unit be activated. It meant I promised to not sue the government if something happened to her while in their care, like a broken leg, loss of eyesight, or death. This form made the paper I signed so she could get her belly button pierced seem like a sales slip for lipstick. I was granting permission for the government I live under and pay taxes to, to use my child's talents and interests for the country's best interests. God help me, the government had better appreciate her.

She'll go to basic training this summer, a complete letting go if there ever was one. If she screws up, it won't be me talking to her about her mistake or grounding her for a night. She'll have a drill sergeant in her face calling her names and screaming at her to do fifty pushups. Instead of her favorite mashed potatoes with cream cheese and sour cream, and Italian chicken drizzled in butter, she'll be eating chipped beef on toast. Instead of sleeping in on warm summer mornings, she'll be up at 4 a.m., running, learning to shoot an M16, and throwing grenades. They'll even put her in a gas chamber. "Cool," she said.

So, I signed it. She'll come home a soldier. A lean, mean fightin' machine. But she'll still be my little girl, and she'll still need me. And my Visa card.

I'm being weaned. Weaned from directing and controlling my girls' destinies. But you know something? When I look at them, when I think of all we've been through, I smile like a Cheshire cat and think, 'Damn, I've done a good job.'

Signing Papers II
Posted September 2009

And I thought signing the papers was hard.

Cassie was seventeen when she joined the Army Reserve. I signed the papers in December 2001 giving the government permission to send my kid through a gas chamber. June 2002 seemed so far away, and nine weeks didn't seem that long. But June soon arrived, and nine weeks became an eternity.

Her grandpa took her to the recruiting station when she left for basic because I knew he'd be stronger than me, and she needed someone to send her off with a smile and some confidence. Dad was in the Navy during the Korean War, so he was just the person to give her the, "You can do it!" pep talk, not her blubbering mother.

I can still bring up that ache in my gut as I hugged her goodbye. She didn't want to go, I didn't want her to go, but a deal is a deal. The worst part for me was knowing I wouldn't hear her voice for at least two weeks. It would be like she landed on the dark side of the moon.

Week two of basic, I brought the cordless phone with me everywhere when I was home and still I missed her first call. I felt like the worst mother in the world. When she finally called back, this was our conversation:

Me: Hello?
Cassie: Mommy?
Me: Cassie? (tears)
Cassie: (tears)
Me: (tears…sniff…sniff)
Cassie: (tears…sniff…sniff)
(This went on, I'm not kidding you, for five minutes.)
Cassie: I have to go. I love you, Mommy. I miss you. (more tears)
Me: I miss you so much, baby. I love you. I love you. (more tears) I'll see you in a few weeks, I promise.

That promise, that I'd see her in a few weeks, I was *not* going to break, despite the fact that I weighed almost three hundred pounds and had stopped going anywhere too far from home. She was in Missouri, and by god, I was going to be there when the Army said she could go home.

I was never so proud of Cassie as I was on Family Day when she marched out with her unit. After the program, and when all the units were dismissed, it took a while to locate her. There were hundreds of people and dozens upon dozens of blond white female soldiers looking for their families, all dressed the same, with their hair tucked in their hats. Somehow, Carlene found her, and I was never so happy to see another human being as I was when I hugged my little-girl-turned-soldier.

I had a hard time walking around the base. My back and knees hurt, and it was ninety-plus degrees. But I downed a bunch of Advil because I wanted to see everything Cassie wanted to show me.

We were allowed to take her off base for the afternoon. She wasn't allowed to shave her legs or underarms, pluck her eyebrows, put on makeup, drink alcohol, smoke, take illegal drugs, or get a tattoo. Good thing none of those things was on our agenda.

We ate lunch, and then I bought her a bathing suit so she could enjoy the pool at the hotel. I was shocked when she put it on. She'd lost a lot of weight, not that she had a lot to lose in the first place.

Exhausted, she was unusually quiet, and after some time at the pool, we went back to our room and slept for three hours.

We took her back to the base, but this goodbye was easy since after graduation the following day, we would take her home.

The next day, we packed her up, and she chose to camp out in the back of the van, sleeping most of the way to Indianapolis. There was one point, though, when I was driving that I looked in the rear-view mirror and saw her making her stuffed bear dance to "Copacabana" playing on the radio. To this day, she still calls that bear "Bear Manilow."

Early the next morning, as Larry and I whispered about our travel plans in the bed next to the girls, Cassie bolted upright, jumped out, and started making the bed with Carlene still sleeping.

I was so surprised that all I could say was, "Honey, honey, it's OK! Sit down. You'll be home today."

She started to cry.

Adjusting to a non-military routine took her a few months, and Cassie's senior year of high school was sometimes lonely. The military had changed her. Basic training gave her a perspective on life, death, and loyalty that many of us, let alone a seventeen-year-old, will never know. The military gave Cassie space to experience the kind of challenge and growth I think she was looking for, even at her young age. While she played the saxophone in marching band, went to prom, and, reluctantly, her graduation, it sometimes seemed like obligatory superficiality.

Cassie lives in Pittsburgh now, and she's creating a life that works for her based on and buoyed by her experiences. The military is still very much in her, yet it does not define who she is.

She still sleeps with Bear Manilow, though.

Twin Daughters of Different Fathers
Posted May 2004

Dan Fogelberg and Tim Weisburg collaborated on an album in 1979 called *Twin Sons of Different Mothers*. It was my favorite nighttime music, and a welcome change from disco. Fogelberg's words and Weisburg's flute both fueled and tamed my angsty sixteen-year-old self. I knew every note, every crescendo, every run. I even taught myself the flute part from the first track, "Twins Theme." Life was full of possibilities. I was going to be either a veterinarian or a roadie for the Eagles. I'd have died laughing if someone told me that instead, within five years, I would produce my own "album": Twin daughters of different fathers.

Never one to do things the conventional way, I turned the old saying, "The first child can come any time, the second one takes nine months" on its ear.

Everyone assumed daughter number one was a guest at her father's and my wedding. Otherwise, why would we have pushed the date up? (Full disclosure: I was, in fact, pregnant when we moved the date up from May 29 to April 3, but I miscarried at eleven weeks.) When Carlene made her appearance three weeks shy of our one-year anniversary, the finger counting had ended and people realized she took the "morally correct" nine months to get here.

For eleven days, we were a happy little family of three. But just as life needs birth, it brings with it death. My farmer husband died, leaving me and our little daughter a family of two. We moved to the city where I went through the motions of life, feeling very little and making choices I wouldn't have otherwise made if not for the constant numbness. It was within this almost hypnotic state that daughter number two came into being.

Cassandre was an actual guest at my second wedding. She was nine months old, teething and crawling, and unaware of the way she turned my world right side up again. Carlene nicknamed her Cassie Bear and liked to hold her like her favorite Cabbage Patch Doll, which in so many ways Cassie was. They became like the Chinese symbol yin-yang: two opposite energies that could not exist without each other. So it was no surprise to me that Carlene moved to Pittsburgh, living as close to Cassie as she could without actually having to share a bathroom.

When Carlene was born, her burgeoning personality was not like anything she'd exhibited *in utero*. A constant kicker and puncher inside, there was no child as quiet and modest as Carlene. Cassie, on the other hand, moved very little, which kept me anxious nearly the entire pregnancy. If not for the hiccups she got nightly, I'd have been at my doctor's office daily wondering if she was alive in there. Once Cassie was out, she hit the ground running and made sure everyone knew she was alive.

Carlene loved to nap. I had to wean her from them a few weeks before she started kindergarten. She still likes to get ten hours of sleep when she can. Cassie, of course, liked being awake, and stopped taking naps at age two simply because, like Bartleby the Scrivener, she preferred not to. She still thrives on motion, and I usually need a nap after spending a day with her.

Everyone has a ratio of book smarts to street smarts. Our ability to think more than feel or feel more than think parlays into our daily lives and influences everything, from the choices we make about which car to buy or clothes to wear, to the jobs we take, the people we choose as friends and lovers, the movies we watch, or the games we play. Mothering two such opposite children gives me a front seat to this psychology. Carlene thinks deeply and methodically. Cassie feels deeply and passionately. Carlene carefully plans. Cassie makes decisions on the fly. Carlene follows directions. Cassie makes up the rules as she goes. Both are independent in very different ways: Carlene stubbornly so and Cassie instinctively so.

Cassie is a defender of the underdog. Carlene prefers justice.

Carlene got A's in calculus, but it took her weeks to learn how to check the oil and fill the windshield wiper fluid tank in our car. Cassie couldn't see what the Pythagorean theorem had to do with her, but she earned enough money from dog sitting, cat sitting, and a paper route to buy a stereo, computer, and television. Cassie instinctively knows things most of us have to learn. The world outside of books makes sense to her, where Carlene would be lost without books.

The girls often flew to Minnesota, Seattle, and Los Angeles to see family. As you might guess, Carlene was an aisle-seat girl and Cassie loved the window. Yet for all her adventurousness, it was Cassie I put in charge of the money and calling card (and her sister, too, for that matter).

Sighing "I'll do it" accompanied by an eye roll was a common occurrence for Cassie, killer of spiders and plunger of toilets. Yet it was Carlene who risked bodily injury to clean Cassie's room while she was at basic training so that Cass had a path to her bed.

Their similarities are what we all want children to be: hard working and kind. They were courteous to my friends and co-workers and, except when Cassie would crawl under the table in restaurants to pull out a loose tooth when she was little, I was never embarrassed to take them out in public.

Carlene never left home easily. Cassie was out the door almost as soon as she got her diploma. That they live in close proximity again makes me happy. I worry less that Carlene will get lost (she has a lousy sense of direction) or that Cassie will be sad (that dominant "feeling" side of her has its downside sometimes).

I found my copy of *Twin Sons of Different Mothers* while writing this column. "Paris Nocturne" is still a lovely song, and it reminds me that the sixteen-year-old I was still lives inside this forty-two-year-old body. At sixteen, I dreamed of becoming a veterinarian, a groupie, a poet, and a pilot, but becoming a mother in a circuitous fashion to two engagingly polar opposites was more heady and humbling than anything I could have ever imagined sitting in my room in the dark, listening to music.

Christmas Invasion
Posted New Year's Day 2007

No one would guess that yesterday there were duffel bags, clothes, shoes, and unwrapped gifts strewn everywhere, and that tiny rubber dental bands dotted the bathroom floor. The Christmas tree is down and all the furniture is back in its place. The hum of electronic games no longer hangs in the air, and the kitchen cupboards are free of Goldfish, Fruit-by-the-Foot, sugared cereal, macaroni and cheese, and anything made by Chef Boyardee. Yet, as my small house breathes a sigh of relief, I feel empty. The stepsons' yearly Christmas invasion is always chaotic and always, always too short.

I realize this isn't a newsflash, but mothering boys is way different than mothering girls. They have dissimilar priorities and interests, and they move through space in diametrically opposing ways in no time at all. It's like a jolt of caffeine one minute and watching paint dry the next. The boys laugh and wrestle and take up the room of what feels like twice the space of their bodies, and then…bam! They switch to single-syllabic answers with their butts plopped on the couch, and hands and eyes glued to a Game Boy.

Kevin at thirteen is very happy that I am now the shortest member of the family. Since August, he has shot up almost an inch in height, which in this small house does not bode well for him. I'm five-foot five-inches and can move easily within the narrow staircases and the low ceilings in the basement, and I don't bump my head on the dormers in the upstairs bedrooms. Andy, who is fifteen and four inches taller, calls the house a death trap for tall people.

The boys walk with every pound of their body in every step. They chew loudly and suck up milk from their bowls like a Saint Bernard, and they regurgitate scenes from *Monty Python and the Holy Grail* at obscure moments throughout the visits.

I'll never understand why combing one's hair and brushing one's teeth is something one needs to be reminded to do every day. They never forget to charge their electronic games and cell phones, but always fail to put the twist tie back on the bread bag or the lid on the jelly jar. They walk the dogs and do various chores when asked—and happily—but dirty underwear lies helplessly balled up in the corner of their room until it can walk to the laundry basket itself.

I roll my eyes at the absurdity, but I'm glad they're boys. They watch movies and listen to music I wouldn't normally choose in my everyday life. With Cherry Garcia ice cream in their bowls and rice cakes in mine, we sat on the couch and watched *Wayne's World* and both Bill & Ted movies. If I'm not called "dude" until I see the boys again this spring, I will be a little sad.

Per Andrew's suggestion, we listened to *The Who's Greatest Hits* while eating Christmas dinner rather than my daughter's suggestion, *Amy Grant Christmas*. It enhanced our "most excellent" meal.

Like all good things, their eight-day visit came to an end. They packed their bags and their Christmas gifts, and we loaded them in the car. We drove three hours to an Arby's in upstate New York where we met their mother, unloaded the car, and hugged our goodbyes. It's every time in that Arby's parking lot that I draw a deep breath and let the emptiness enter. It settles in, acutely at first, and then moves to the back of my mind where it coexists with the other emotions of my life.

During their visits, we live an unconscious cycle: I mother them the best way I can and they teach me how to be a better mother. I can live with that. Just as I can live with a quiet house and that brief moment of emptiness. They'll be back.

And maybe it will be their next visit that they remember to brush their teeth.

Date Night
Posted February 2007

My probably-gay ex-boyfriend did little for me except break my heart in 1996, but he did turn me on to Toad the Wet Sprocket. My love of Toad continues, as does, sometimes, the deep dislike of the old boyfriend.

My daughter Carlene serendipitously found out that Toad's lead singer, Glen Phillips was performing in Pittsburgh and she asked if I wanted to go. As an early birthday gift to her, I bought us tickets, and we headed to Club Café on the South Side.

Club Café is an intimate little club with a small stage, perfect for acoustic performers. We stood at the end of the bar near the front door because all the seats were taken by the time we arrived. We scoped the crowd of mostly thirty- and forty-year-olds. Carlene was probably the youngest at almost twenty-four. The bartender, who looked like Cameron Diaz, poured us some wine. We ordered a couple of salads and artichoke dip and talked about how this was our first time in a club together.

There was a tall bearded man sitting behind the bouncers and paying attention to a laptop. In front of the computer was a stack of Glen Phillips CDs for sale, as well as CDs by a guy named Craig Cardiff. I turned back to the bar and took a sip of wine when I spied Glen out of the corner of my eye walking toward the tall bearded guy behind me. The two of them chatted for a minute before the tall bearded man walked away.

I'd brought along my copy of Glen's solo album, *Abulum*, and with a glass of wine in me, I asked him if I could "bother him for an autograph." I, of course, babbled on like a typical enamored fan about how I loved his music and brought up my children listening to it, blah, blah, blah, all the while telling myself in my head to shut up, but I didn't, and he was gracious and signed the liner notes and thanked me.

A few minutes later, the tall bearded man walked on to the stage with a guitar strapped to his back. He wasn't Glen's lighting guy. He was, in fact, Craig Cardiff, and the moment he started to play, my love affair with the tall bearded man's music began. Later, I got his autograph, too, and I talked to him as the real me and not the silly blithering idiot that came out when I talked to Glen.

Glen's set was excellent. He has an intimate rapport with the audience, too. When he asked if anyone had listened to last week's *Wait, Wait, Don't Tell Me!*, I, of course, clapped and yelled, "Yes! Woohoo!" I was the only person in the club to do so. (I'm a *Wait, Wait...* junkie, and my dream is to one day win Carl Kasell's voice on my answering machine. It's not every day I'm in a bar and someone brings up my favorite

NPR show, you know?) Even though this was a slightly embarrassing moment, this seemed to please Glen, and maybe it made up for our conversation earlier.

Glen sang some of his solo songs and a few Toad songs, and for an hour, I was immersed in a familiar voice from my past. Not once did I associate it with the ex-boyfriend. Major victory for me.

Carlene linked her arm with mine for the last few songs and we sang with the crowd. This was her growing-up music; a perfect concert for mother-daughter bar bonding. Classy, yet comfortably fun.

Shopping and the (Reluctant) Teenage Boy
Posted July 2007

Three young kids on the corner of our street are selling makeovers.

You read that right.

Every time a car or pedestrian goes by, they yell out, "Makeovers! Fifteen cents!"

I wonder if they could help my fourteen-year-old stepson. Kevin needs a makeover. He doesn't care if his hair is combed or his teeth are brushed or that he's outgrown his pants and looks ready for a flood. As long as he has his Game Boy and the TV remote control, the boy is happy. Wait, I forgot the beef jerky. He's happiest eating beef jerky, too.

I took Kevin shopping yesterday to spend his birthday gift cards. We went to Best Buy first. At Best Buy, Kevin is in his element. He could spend hours ogling the merchandise and playing games. But Kevin also had another gift card to spend. One that, when it popped out of his birthday card, made him turn white as a sheet.

All his life, new clothes have magically appeared in his room. Kevin never had to go shopping, never had to try on anything in a dressing room. His mother knew his sizes and bought what she thought was appropriate. If it didn't fit, she returned it. That's fine for her, but that's not how I roll. The boy needed new clothes, and the only way he was going to get them was by going shopping. With me.

When we walked into Old Navy, I asked him what size he was. He shrugged his shoulders and said, "Iontknow," all one word, just like that. I made him turn around, and I pulled out the tag of his jeans. 14 Regular. It was a place to start.

"What kind of shorts do you need?" I asked.

"Iontknow," he said, looking through the rack. He held out a price tag. "They're kinda expensive."

Bless his heart.

"Kevin, that's cheap," I laughed, looking at the tag. "Trust me. Pick something out."

He spied a pair of khakis. They had to go past his knees, he explained, otherwise everyone at school would tease him for wearing "short shorts." I sighed and grabbed a pair of non-short shorts and asked him what kind of shirt he wanted. Polo? "Iontknow." I gave him a look and directed him to the shirts. He looked around and pointed at a blue striped polo. I grabbed one in what I figured was his size and we headed to the dressing room.

"Do you need t-shirts?" I asked as we passed a sale table. "They're only $3.25."

Again, a shrug. We got to the dressing room and he followed the attendant to a room. She said to let her know if he needed anything, and he looked at her like she'd asked him to strip naked and lie on an ant hill.

In the time it would take me to try on a dress, three pairs of pants, and two strapless bras, Kevin tried on a shirt. Thank god it fit and he liked it.

"Do the shorts fit?" I asked five minutes later.

"Um, no," he grunted in his best voice-changed baritone.

"Would you like me to get you a different size?" I offered, knowing that if the dressing room attendant asked him, he'd be eaten alive by those ants.

"Um, yeah."

I brought him a larger size and he tried them on. At least I assume he tried them on. He didn't model them. When he opened the dressing room door, he was dressed in his own clothes, and he had both pairs of shorts meticulously hung back on the hanger.

We walked out of the dressing room and past the t-shirts again.

"Um, I'm going to camp, and you know, you can't have enough dry t-shirts," Kevin said.

I smiled.

"Pick out two in a medium, OK?" I told him.

At the checkout, I gave him twenty dollars to cover whatever his gift card didn't. He rolled the bill nervously around in his hand as the clerk scanned his items, then he threw it on the counter when she announced the total.

"Kev," I sighed, "at least unroll the bill and hand it to her."

"Oh," he said, and reached for the bill. The cashier laughed and picked it up as it was. I just shook my head.

Baby steps. Today, he survived shopping. Tomorrow…well, maybe those makeover kids on the corner have some ideas.

Music, Movies, and the (Reluctant) Stepmother
Posted July 2007

The best part of Kevin's shopping trip yesterday, according to Kevin, was buying a video game and Weird Al's CD, *Running with Scissors*. He could have bought the CD used on Amazon for four bucks, but nope. He wanted to torture us all the way home from Pittsburgh.

I like a good Weird Al parody once in a while. I mean, I have a sense of humor. "Like A Surgeon," "Another One Rides the Bus," "Eat It." No doubt the man is funny. Listening to an entire album though, takes more patience than watching paint dry. I made it twenty-five miles before I took out my stepmother voice and said, "Enough!" and ejected the CD. The song "Albuquerque" alone is eleven minutes long! That's a lot of Weirdness, my friends.

There's always some alternative education going on when the stepsons visit. They show me a world this mother of girls has never seen before. I won't admit this to him, but I'm kind of glad Kevin introduced me to the music of the Arrogant Worms. I laughed out loud when I heard "Ontario Sucks." Just don't tell him I said that.

During this visit, I also learned there is a very important difference between a nerd and a geek. I called Kevin a geek after he described a dance some guy did on a weirdass television show that only teenage boys watch, and he promptly corrected me saying he was actually a nerd. Both geeks and nerds are super smart, he said, but nerds have friends. Oh. OK. I apologized, and promised to refer to him in the future as a nerd since he assured me he has friends, all of whom have apparently seen the movie *Borat*—a movie his mother, father, and I all agree Kevin does *not* need to see, and especially not at fourteen. It doesn't matter, though. He can quote every scene, thanks to his nerd friends. Imagine, if you will, a room full of Kevins quoting *Borat*. Oh dear god, hell is surely less painful.

Every visit is a new adventure, and when Kevin and his brother are here again in August—this time for two weeks—they will no doubt give me something new to write about.

Common Ground

The Yin & Yang of Stepparenting
Posted August 2007

I write a lot about my stepsons, and usually with a lighthearted pen. But the truth is, stepparenting is hard, and until now, while I've hinted at it, I've not written it out loud.

Even after eleven years, I feel like strangers move into my house several weeks a year. Strangers being raised in a far different environment than if they lived with their father and me full time. The lifestyle they embrace, and the priorities and expectations of their mother are not the same as ours, and I'm torn between feeling sorry for them for being lobbed between these diverse environments and feeling sorry for myself for having to repeat our rules and expectations every time they're here. We want them to: chew with their mouths shut, use Kleenex and not their sleeves, brush their teeth, take showers (and not the fifteen-minute kind), eat fruit and vegetables, think about people other than themselves, and tell us more about their thoughts on the world and life and less about how many people they kill or blow up on a video game.

I realize much of their behavior is typical of teenaged boys and not a stepparenting issue per se, but the difficulty with parenting the boys a few weeks and a few long weekends a year as opposed to most of the time is that when they visit, we start over. Every time. There's a surge, a wave, that crashes in the door when they arrive—bags and chaos and nonstop talking, each trying to tell us their stories over each other. There's no natural rhythm, and on those rare occasions when we get them for longer than a few weeks and we start to establish a routine, they leave. Then in a few months, it starts all over again.

What I've learned is that, to keep up, we have to prepare—physically and especially emotionally—for their visits; dust off that parenting hat, put it on, and get ready for the wave.

They'll be here in nine hours. As I write this, I remember how their mother told me several years ago that I'm not a "real" parent to the boys, a classic stepparenting cliché. I did not give birth to or adopt the boys, therefore I am irrelevant. I realize now that she most likely spoke those words out of fear, but they pissed me off. I refuse to treat the boys as my friends, and have always had the same expectation of them as I do my biological children. They are a part of our family and as such, they must do their part to maintain the integrity of our family. It took a while, but I'm super proud that they do the dishes when asked and don't complain. They pick up the dog poop and don't complain. They are good travelers and don't complain.

Even though it's non-stop doing and talking the minute they walk in the house, and there is no quiet unless they're sleeping or playing a video game or reading, and overall their presence is heavy in our small house, I love the boys like a "real" parent.

Twelve Hours Later…

This morning, my underwear was all in a bunch as I prepared for (and somewhat dreaded) the boys' tsunami arrival. Then, when they got here, it was like they were just here, and I remembered why I love it when they visit.

We had a great evening. My head's on straight. I'm ready to be the mom they know me to be — fun, yet not afraid to tell them what's what. (Lucky me got to answer Kevin's question: What's a blow job?)

Good times are ahead. Stressful times, too, I'm sure. But when the stress happens, we'll deal with it. We always do. We're a good little family that way.

So far there have been no snorting nose issues. Andy shared the videos he made at video camp (yes, there is such a thing—who knew?). Larry and I are really proud of his work. Kevin told us about Boy Scout camp and it was a little heart wrenching. The older boys were idiots and called him a wimp when he pulled a tendon in his knee. As strong as Kevin is, he had a hard time dealing with their ridicule. I got all puffy-chested and mom-like and wanted to go slap those stupid boys and say horrible things to them. Anyway, I'm glad Kevin felt loved enough to reveal what he was feeling.

I love the boys and I love being their stepmother. The house is full, and so is my heart.

A Not-So-Martha-Stewart Thanksgiving
Posted November 2007

I listen to a lot of Martha Stewart Living on Sirius radio, so much so that I'm feeling impotent this Thanksgiving. I don't make a centerpiece from kumquats and pinecones. My stuffing is made from pre-sliced, store-bought bread, not homemade. And I didn't raise my own sweet potatoes fertilized by the droppings of rare Amazon parrots.

Martha slaughters her own turkey. I buy one at the grocery store. At least this year I bought a free-range organic turkey at Whole Foods. It's a step up, right?

Party Potatoes, I'm sure, won't be on Martha's table this year. They are an artery-clogging combination of butter, sour cream, and cream cheese that completely negate the nutritional value of potatoes. Party Potatoes are so far removed from being a vegetable that they could be classified as dairy.

When my girls were little, I always made enough Party Potatoes for Thanksgiving so they could have them for breakfast the next morning. One year, my youngest daughter got up early and took the lion's share of leftover potatoes before her sister woke up. This led to a screaming match and tears.

"They're just potatoes," I said, laughing at their tirade.

"No, they're not!" my oldest daughter fired back. "They're *Party Potatoes*! You don't understand!"

Clearly I didn't.

My stepsons aren't fans of Party Potatoes. My daughters tease them for preferring plain mashed potatoes, like it's some kind of embarrassing fetish.

Martha might be amused by our "Black Olives Over the Eyes" photo we take each Thanksgiving. Many years ago, my little sister held black olives up to her eyes while I was taking a picture of the Thanksgiving feast and the tradition was born. Every year, my girls, stepsons, and any other "child" at our table, pose for this classic photo.

No one in the photo actually likes black olives, and so they put them back on the relish tray before I have a chance to ask if they've washed their hands. It's kind of gross now that I think about it. How many unsuspecting dinner guests have eaten black olives that earlier had been placed over the eyes of children? Please don't report me to the Martha Stewart etiquette police.

My favorite part of Thanksgiving is when we sit down at the table about a half hour before the food is ready, and we each pray out loud what we're grateful for. The only rule is that it has to be more meaningful than just grunting, "Thanks for the food." Kevin bets me a dollar every year that I'll cry when it comes my turn to pray. I've not won a bet yet.

This year, as always, I'm grateful for my home and my family. In particular, I am grateful for my new granddaughter, friends old and new, and the opportunities that have sprung from difficulty, namely my arthritis issues. I'm grateful for the pain; it has been an invaluable teacher. I'm grateful for the anguish; it has kept my feet on the ground.

This year, I learned over and over that good can come from bad and that it doesn't just happen. I am an active participant in my present and future.

I wish you all a very happy and peaceful Thanksgiving. Surround yourself with the people who make you happy. That's something Martha and I agree on.

I Need to Be Needed
Posted December 2007

I might be an empty nester, but I'm still the mom with everything.

My oldest daughter was home this weekend because she's in a wedding. While getting ready for the rehearsal dinner, she realized she forgot her razor. And she had a hole in her stockings. And the shoes she brought weren't suited for her outfit. And she didn't have a lighter jacket than her winter coat. And the batteries in her camera were losing power.

That's where I always come in. I'm never without an extra razor or two, and the junk drawer is stocked with batteries. Carlene and I wear the same size stockings and shoes, and I had a sweater that she could wear and not be bogged down by a heavy coat.

When the kids visit and forget a toothbrush? Mom's got an extra. Forget deodorant? Mom has both roll-on and aerosol. Need to ship a package? Mom's got boxes and tape and a postal scale. Cold? There are always plenty of jackets, mittens, boots, and hats. When my girls don't have quite the right shirt or skirt, they know I probably do.

My purse is *Let's Make a Deal* ready. I've got Band-Aids, a nail file, Tic Tacs, two kinds of gum, retail "member" cards from every major store, paper, pens, pencils, a two-dollar bill, lipstick, lip gloss, dental floss, hand lotion, a compact, comb, aspirin, Celebrex, Xanax, antacids,

Kleenex, vitamins, postage stamps, and God knows what else you'll find if you dig deep enough.

You'd think I was a pack rat, but I'm not. I don't hang on to things that I won't use within a reasonable amount of time. In fact, I'm prone to throwing things or giving things away, before realizing a short time later that I need them. I think it's just years of practice that keeps me in supply of useful things just beyond the scope of every day. Why have one screwdriver when three or four in varying sizes have more potential uses? One curling iron is a good thing, but a collection of one half-inch iron, one one-inch iron, and a flat iron is even better. If you have straight hair, I have shampoo for that. Curly hair? Yup. Got that, too.

My pantry and refrigerator always have enough food for unexpected company or for days when I don't feel like making the meal I'd planned. I hate running out of cooking spray, so I pick up a can when I think of it at the grocery store. Same with dog treats and sweet potatoes. They keep, they're cheap, and I avoid running out at a time when I need them the most. (Not that one *needs* sweet potatoes.)

I like being the mom with everything. When your kids leave home, you still want them to need you in some capacity, right? I'm glad my daughter could wear my shiny black boots last Friday. I'm glad I had a razor she could use and stockings to wear and a sweater. Having batteries on hand saved her a trip to the store, preventing her from rushing to the rehearsal dinner.

They'll all be here in a few days for Christmas. I'm sure there will be something they've forgotten or realize they need. I'm ready. I bought a few extra toothbrushes at the store today. I've got plenty of laundry soap, a Clorox pen, gift wrap, tape and scissors, and extra blankets and slippers in case it gets cold. I always tell them, if I don't have it, you probably don't need it.

The Boys Are Back in Town
Posted April 2008

I can see them but they can't see me, my teenage stepsons who just arrived with their father a few minutes ago. They are sitting outside on the deck. It's spring break and they will be here for the week. Time to dust off my mothering skills and get to it.

They both tower over me now, my once small boys who'd crawl up on my lap and tell me stories or watch TV with me. Now they lay sprawled on the couch and an overstuffed chair playing hand-held video games.

Their father has to work while they're here, so the boys and I will go to Pittsburgh to see their niece, sisters, and brother-in-law for a few days.

Our car trips are always memorable. We sing and Kevin plays air guitar or air drums. Problem is, he doesn't realize how tall and lanky he's become. If he's in the front seat, his arms flail into my driving space, and if he's in the back, he kicks the back of my seat like he did when he was little. He doesn't mean to, and he always apologizes with an "Oops! Sorry!" accompanied by a short deep giggle. (I'm still not used to his voice change.)

Car time is also a good time to just catch up. We email and talk on the phone in between visits, but when we get to see each other for real, and especially when I get them alone in a moving vehicle and they can't escape, I ask the most detailed questions I can. On the phone, they grunt answers to their father's questions, but they know I need plain English. When we go to Pittsburgh, we'll talk about school and their friends, but I think mostly I'll ask them about what girls are in their lives, both as friends and as possible more-than-friends. They'll blush, but I can usually get them to talk.

And if I can't, their sisters can.

A highlight this week for their dad will be taking Andy out driving.

Andy will get his permit soon. I know he's sixteen and very tall, but to see him behind the wheel of a car? I'm not sure I'm ready for that. He said he might even go to prom this year. Yikes! Good lord, I'll be a wreck when he graduates from high school in 2010. You'd think I birthed the boy. Sometimes it feels like I did. I've known him almost as long.

The week will go by too fast. There will be fart jokes and booger jokes, and I'll have to remind them to use Kleenex and to put their underwear in the hamper. But as I've written before, as stressful as it can be at times, I love our two-thirds of a Brady Bunch family.

I only wish we had our own Alice.

Mother's Day Music
Posted May 2009

My daughters spend weeks every year putting together my Mother's Day present. To them, Mother's Day is bigger than Christmas or my birthday.

This year, they compiled a CD of songs that reminded them of me and us and the hard times and the good times of their growing up, when I questioned almost everything I did as a parent. Was I too lenient? Too stern? Did I tell them too much? Not enough? I look at them sometimes—they are smart, kind, and a lot of fun—and I wonder, "Where the heck did you girls come from?"

Their note: Hi Mom! OK, we put together a few of our memories of the songs on your CD. Some songs are kind of cheesy and from the '80s, but they are songs that have stuck out in our heads since we were little kids. I don't think the memories are in the CD's order, but I'm sure you'll figure it out. xoxox

Common Ground

"Got My Mind Set on You" — George Harrison

Carlene: Some of my favorite memories of Mom is when we'd watch this music video. It always cracked me up watching the moose head on the wall dancing and such. I always think of Cassie dancing her little knee-bopping dance as a little kid listening to this song and watching the video.

"Bohemian Rhapsody" — Queen

Carlene: I remember when Mom picked me up from the airport. We were driving on the highway and this song came on the radio. I had no other memory of being *so* incredibly happy to be home, so Mom cranked this song up and we sang it at the top of our lungs while doing our version of head banging. With Mom it was always OK to act a little strange. We kept laughing harder as we'd see the people in other cars look at us like we were nuts.

"Copacabana" — Barry Manilow

Cassie: Personally, for me, this song makes me very happy. When driving home after ten long weeks of being away at basic training, Mom bought me a little bear that I named Bear Manilow because half asleep in the very back of the van, I made it dance to this song. We were all laughing so hard, I think we were all in tears. Even Larry! I had never been so happy to be with my family at that moment.

Lynn Haraldson

"Good Things"—BoDeans

Cassie: This song reminds me of when the three of us drove to Minnesota for Grandpa's birthday. I remember when everyone else was tired, I popped this CD (the live one) in, and Mom and I sang to it while Carly slept in the back. We also got some good chatting in, too, as always.

Carlene: I wouldn't have my appreciation of the BoDeans if Mom hadn't had them on all the time. Such great music and always a favorite when I'd raid Mom's CD collection (which I did frequently!). The BoDeans bring me back to about ages ten to thirteen. Tough times during those years, but also wonderful times that brought us so close.

"Galileo"—Indigo Girls

Cassie: Nothing reminds me more of Mom than Indigo Girls. Frankie, too. Those were the good days. We would all hang out with music in the background. I can still hear it playing when we'd take any sort of road trip in PA. Didn't we listen to it on the way to Gettysburg?

Carlene: I remember stealing this tape from you for a long time. Who knows if I ever gave it back! Like Cassie said, this also reminds me of Frankie and the play she put together based on *Wuthering Heights* and I played Heathcliff. Every time I hear an Indigo Girls song today I think of Mom.

"Wide Open Spaces" — Dixie Chicks

Cassie: For me, this song reminds me of my wedding. Mom wouldn't tell me what song we'd dance to, so when this song came on, I had a feeling I already knew she'd choose this one… Simply because it fit for us and how we are. Mom has always let me be the free spirit I am, and she never made me feel like I had to apologize for it or conform to everyone else. She's always let me be me, and that's what a good Mom is all about.

Carlene: I, too, think of Cassie's wedding when I hear this song. Again, Mom's country music collection was small, but the Dixie Chicks made the cut! I actually think of going off to college to Bloomsburg and saying goodbye to both Mom and Cassie with this song. That was a huge time in my life and I missed Mom and Cassie terribly. Mom always let us be our own people and stretch our legs and be who we needed to be.

"I'll Stand by You" — The Pretenders

Cassie: I don't have a specific memory for this song, but I do remember Mom always saying she loved this song. However, when I do think of this song, it takes me back to a sad time in Minnesota, and how we were all there for each other to get through it.

Carlene: This song make me think of the three of us. We'll all stand by each other no matter what. Enough said.

"Fire and Rain" — James Taylor

Carlene: I could always count on Mom to listen to good mellow James Taylor. This was always one I remember playing.

Cassie: I wouldn't have my appreciation for classic rock and James Taylor if it wasn't for Mom. Gosh, we've been listening to James Taylor since I was a tiny kid. I can't remember a time when we *didn't* listen to James Taylor!

"Landslide" — Fleetwood Mac

Cassie: I know this song is more for Carly, being as Mom wrote about it when she was graduating from college. But for me, this song is more on a Mom level. I would sing this song a lot to Claire when she was a little baby to calm her. It always worked. As a mother, this song's lyrics are both sad and hopeful, thinking about how wonderful it is to love someone/something so much. However, as they grow (which is wonderful), you are also growing and getting older. For me, I always think of how Mom would say she virtually grew up with us, and now as a mother, I'm doing the same thing. So as the lyrics go, "I've been afraid of changing 'cause I built my life around you…"

Carlene: This is a beautiful song and it always reminds me of Mom. Even though Stevie Nicks says, "this one's for you Daddy," I think of Mom.

"Alone" — Heart

Cassie: Do I really have to say anything? It's Heart! And this is the best Heart song ever!

Carlene: LOL, Cassie! I don't know about the best Heart song EVER, but it is a good one. (Too bad Celine Dion had to butcher it with a cover!) I fell in love with Heart partially because Mom listened to Heart. And these chicks rock!

"Have a Little Faith in Me" — John Hyatt

Cassie: Not only is this one of the best songs EVER, but this and the Jewel version were often played in the house and car. It's one of those songs you can listen to and just feel good all over knowing that someone feels this way about you.

Carlene: This is a great song and it reminds me of Mom. I think the Jewel version is from the *Phenomenon* soundtrack, which I know made Mom cry! There are times when the three of us just know to keep having faith in each other. If we didn't, we wouldn't be as close as we are today. This song symbolizes that perfectly.

"Begin" — Toad the Wet Sprocket

Cassie: Talk about a depressing song. But I remember on many occasions Mom mentioned how this song reminded her of me. I do think that past the sad parts of the song, it's about a child being wiser than its age and maybe that's how Mom felt about me at the time?

Carlene: Yes, I think of Mom and Cassie with this song, but overall Toad reminds me of Mom. Getting to see Glen Phillips on my birthday at Club Café was the best gift from Mom. True, I got a little tipsy, but the concert was still amazing. I'm so glad Mom loves Toad!

"I'm the Only One" — Melissa Etheridge

Carlene: Cassie forgot all about this song until I reminded her. I always think of Mom with this song because we went to the Melissa Etheridge concert at the Target Center together. That was such a fun time sitting in the VIP suite!

"Freedom" — George Michael

Carlene: George Michael always reminds me of Mom. My earliest memory is of Wham and "Wake me up Before You Go Go"! I was probably only four or five when that song came out. Even after Wham, Mom still listened to George Michael, and therefore he makes me think of her.

Other songs the girls selected but made no comment about include: "Ice Cream" by Sarah McLachlan; "Look Heart, No Hands" by Randy Travis; "Thing Called Love" by Bonnie Raitt; "Dancy's Dream" by Restless Heart; and "She's in Love with the Boy" by Trisha Yearwood.

They know me so well.

Screw up as we might as mothers, daughters, sisters, friends, whatever — we're loved and remembered in ways we don't realize or we've forgotten.

Blackbird Revisited
Posted March 2012

You were sixteen when you told me I was your best friend.

"Well, thank you, honey. But..." I hesitated. "You're not my friend."

You did what I thought you'd do. You gave me that look. You know the one where you lower your chin and scrunch up your eyebrows and blow out a sharp, short breath through your nose? No one does that look like you.

"I don't tell my friends when to come home at night," I continued, "and I don't ground them when they've done something wrong. I don't buy them food or wash their clothes, either. I'm glad you think of me as a friend, but I'd rather be your mom."

Thirteen years later, I'm still your mom. But a funny thing happened on the way to this eve of your twenty-ninth birthday.

You became my friend.

Remember when we drove home from D.C. via I-68 because you and your sister had never been to West Virginia? We sang Chrissie Hynde songs, and talked and laughed and didn't notice we were climbing a mountain, even though our ears were popping. That's how this daughter-friend thing developed: slowly and steadily, year after year, built unassumingly on the foundation of the amazingality that is you. (I made up a word for your birthday!)

You've always spoken with the wisdom of someone older, no matter your age. This has served our relationship well.

I was not encouraged to speak my truth as I grew up, so I was always a little intimidated and awed when you did. Like the time you were three and I sent you to your room for a time out. You stood at the top of the stairs, hands on your hips, and yelled "Mommy! You piss me off!" I was stunned. But I smiled and shook my head and thought, "I'm doing something right."

Then there was the time when you were ten and your stepfather and I had a fight on the phone. After I hung up, I smacked the phone into the cradle until it broke. I probably swore some, too. You walked up to me and (speaking for your sister as well) said calmly, "Mom, when you get mad and yell like that, it scares us."

That simple statement of fact, and the calmly passionate way in which you said it, gave rise to one of the greatest challenges of my life. I may not always hold my tongue, but your words started me on a path to a greater awareness of my expression of anger.

I know you aren't comfortable defending yourself to others who have wronged you, and so your voice of truth is often limited to our family. However, rather than seek revenge, you plot forgiveness. That is a gift from your father. When someone asks me to describe him, I tell them, "He was a lot like Carlene." Anyone who believes nurture determines a child's destiny hasn't watched you grow up within the nature of your father. I nurtured you, but you are not me. At least, not the restless, wandering, quick-tempered me.

You at age twenty nine are far different than me at twenty nine. When I turned twenty nine, you were nine and your sister was seven. I'd been married three times—widowed once, divorced twice—and was dating someone seven years younger than me, and on that birthday, I got a tattoo.

You have a clean marital record and no tattoos. Not that there's anything wrong with tattoos. But there was that tongue piercing you got that I never understood. That was definitely something I'd have done, not something I ever thought you'd do.

You inherited your great-grandmother's table, buffet, and dishes at a much younger age than I did because, unlike me, you didn't spend years drifting from apartment to apartment. Nice dishes and buffets require commitment, and—as you know—since your father died, commitment is not easy for me.

I don't write these things with regret. I wouldn't change the path I chose after he died. Like you, I chose what suited me and my circumstances at the time. Your path suits your laid back demeanor just as mine suits my tenuous affair with uncertainty. Where I am impulsive, you are contemplative. Where I am quick to anger, you are cautiously optimistic. I love to compete; you love to knit. I have blue eyes and yours are brown. I wouldn't wish it any other way.

When you left home, you didn't leave me behind. In the years since you've become an adult, you've talked me down and talked me up. You've stayed open minded when I haven't made the best decisions. We've shared millions of words over gallons of coffee and wine. We've rolled our eyes and cried over copious amounts of breakfast foods and salads. A few years ago, after knee surgery, you helped me through my greatest physical pain, and I trusted you implicitly when you said, "It will be OK, Mommy."

Happy birthday, my daughter-friend, my snark-sister, my confidant. I love you more than you can ever know.

In the Fight of His Life
Posted July 2020

I didn't have this on my 2020 Apocalypse Bingo Card. Last week, my twenty-eight-year-old stepson Andrew had a stroke.

While this isn't my story to tell, and Andrew is an extremely private person, I want to raise awareness of a form of vasculitis called granulomatosis with polyangiitis (GPA), formerly known as Wegener's. GPA is a rare disorder characterized by inflammation of the blood vessels, which can restrict blood flow and damage vital organs and tissues. Besides potential damage to the kidneys and respiratory tract, other serious complications may include vision or hearing loss, heart disease, and stroke. There is no cure, and patients with GPA will experience remission and relapse throughout their lifetime.

We don't know how Andrew contracted this rare disease that affects just three in one hundred thousand people, but since July 2019, it has nearly cost him his life three times.

I have known Andrew since he was one and have been his and his brother Kevin's stepmother since 1996. When his father and I divorced, we agreed that our blended family would remain the most important thing in our lives and we have honored that agreement for nearly ten years.

The last time I saw Andrew was a few weeks before Christmas. He and Kevin met me for brunch in Pittsburgh on their way home from visiting their father. Larry and Kevin tried to prepare me for how Andrew's appearance had changed, but I was shocked to see my tall and once incredibly fit boy so thin and pale. His usually robust appetite was reduced to a bit of yogurt and granola. That night, after their long drive back to central New York, Andrew was in renal failure. He has been on dialysis ever since and is on the list for a kidney transplant.

The stroke has set back that timetable, however. Right now, there are more pressing physical issues that he needs to address like learning to speak clearly again and walking unassisted. His mental health needs attention, too. While Andrew has maintained his sense of humor through much of this, he is frustrated and afraid. He is unable to work and is on long-term disability. Because of covid-19, he has no real social life. If not for his cat, Zelda, he would be completely alone most of the time. We can't visit him in person, although his father, mother, and brother have been allowed to see him for a few minutes each day in the hospital this week.

I love both of my stepsons so much, and to see one of them suffering like this is incredibly heartbreaking. But thank you for reading. It helps knowing others are listening.

Epilogue

While Andrew is still recovering and, given the nature of his disease, always will be, he remains upbeat and hopeful. Prior to his illness, he graduated from film school and, like all starving artists, worked outside his field to make the rent. His love for movies and filmmaking gives him purpose and hope during these difficult times. Andrew is an extremely private person, so I asked him to read this chapter before I published it. I wanted to know if he was comfortable with the selections that included him being in the public again (since these were all published in my column in the newspaper). Not only was he comfortable, he loved the trip down memory lane.

Kevin surprised us all when, in 2011, the night before he was to move into a dorm at Utica College, he announced he wanted to be an auto mechanic instead of majoring in science. When I really think about it, though, none of us should have been surprised. He built his first rocket when he was eight years old and his science-leaning brain never shuts off. He reads voraciously and widely, and while we don't see eye-to-eye on some political issues, he is always respectful. We text frequently and see each other every Christmas, and he always remembers to call me on Mother's Day, Thanksgiving, and my birthday.

Cassie, as you will read in the next chapter, is married and has four children. She was discharged from the Army Reserve due to a broken hip and went on to become a nurse. She currently stays home with the kids, teaches fitness classes and is a personal trainer. It's no surprise to me that she volunteers for a number of organizations and raises money for kids in need. Kindness and empathy are as natural to her as breathing.

Carlene is married and works for the defense department. She remained close to Bruce's parents the rest of their lives. She still has her father's eyes and his smile, and I sometimes shed a tear or two when I look at her too long. Her father would be as proud of her as I am, and my wish has never changed, that I hope wherever his spirit dwells, he can look at her once in a while and know he lives on.

4. On Being a Grandparent

"There must be some pheromone, some chemistry that marks the entry into grandparenthood, opening up new emotional spaces… (My grandchildren) have already taught me how small the world and how wide open the future is."

—Ellen Goodman

Before my first grandchild, Claire, was born, there were two moments when I gave any thought to becoming a grandparent, and both scared the bejesus out of me.

The first was when my oldest daughter got her first period, two weeks shy of her twelfth birthday.

"This means I can have a baby, right?" she said matter-of-factly over breakfast.

I choked on my coffee.

"Well, yes, technically," I said. "But don't for a long time, OK?"

The second time, my youngest daughter came into my office one evening and sat down. She'd been crying.

"I need to tell you something," she said softly. My heart dropped. She was sixteen and had been dating someone for a year. Until that moment, I was fairly certain they hadn't had sex, but that's the first place my brain went: *She's going to tell me she's pregnant. What do I do? What do I say? Am I mad? How will I tell my parents? My parents? Really? Get it together, Lynn!*

What she told me instead was far different, something that probably would have made hearing about a pregnancy easier to understand. While that is not my story to tell, I can say that thankfully, in time, Cassie worked through the issue, and it was several years later and at the right time in her life (and, selfishly, mine) that she told me she was pregnant.

Learning of Claire's existence challenged me to be OK with what I didn't know yet, and taught me how to sit with anticipation and not try to fix it.

I have four grandchildren now. With each one I relearned how to not project how I might feel before I felt it and to not plan or anticipate the way I think things will or should be. In this approach to them, and to life in general, I experience my grandchildren where they are in the moment, even those, or perhaps *especially* those moments that aren't all rainbows and unicorns.

See You in October!
Posted March 2007

You're no bigger than a walnut, but you're my favorite kid on the planet.

If all is going well in there, you have the beginnings of hands, feet, ears, kidneys, a liver, and a brain. Somewhere along your journey, I hope you also develop a good sense of humor. You'll need it in this family.

I learned of your existence in a way only your mama would do. We were meeting at Applebee's for lunch. I was seated, but your mom wasn't there yet, only she was, just not in the dining room. She came out of the bathroom and dropped something on my menu.

"Am I reading this right?" she asked.

It took me a few seconds to realize it was a completed pregnancy test. I picked up the stick, and there seemed to be a faint blue plus sign in the middle of the center hole. It was hard to tell.

"I...I don't know," I stuttered.

Mechanically and without much emotion, we spent lunch reading the instructions over and over, making sure we were, in fact, seeing a blue plus sign. It was one of those things we wanted to be true, but we didn't dare hope too hard just in case. Once we were fairly certain that you were, indeed, in there, we got happy and called your Aunt Carlene from your mom's car.

It's taking time for this news to sink in, but I do know this: You and I are going to have a good time. I'll teach you to make lefse and bird seed cakes, and I will read you all my favorite children's books. We'll stay up past your bedtime because we've made a tent in the living room. We'll eat s'mores by flashlight, and listen to Raffi and sing "Baby Beluga," just like I did with your mama and Auntie Carly (do you like that name better?).

You will be adored by many, but I'm the only Grandma Lynn you'll ever have, and I already adore you like no one else. You are my future of wonder and anticipation, happiness and hope. Just the thought of you, I know a new kind of love that is untethered to the responsibilities of parenthood. Discipline will be negotiable.

I don't care if you get your dad's bad sinuses or your mom's bad hips, my lack of coordination or your grandpa's taste in music. We'll work through it. Just come out screaming and everything will be fine.

See you in October, little one. Stay inside until every last cell you need is in place. I'll be here, waiting to welcome you to the other side.

Lynn Haraldson

Buoyant
Posted August 2007

Ever since I learned that Grandbaby will arrive in October, experienced grandparents have tried to share with me what it feels like to be a grandparent. They all say pretty much the same thing: it's hard to explain.

I suspect it's like describing the color blue to someone who has never seen blue. Each of us who've seen the color blue relate to it differently. Anyone who hasn't seen blue can read elaborate descriptions and poetry and chemical analyses of blue, but until they experience blue themselves, they can do little more than shrug their shoulders and trust (or not) that blue is what everyone else says it is.

Here at the end of month seven of this journey between zygote and breathing, I sometimes float in waves of feelings—some sweet, some frightening, and some so deeply awe striking they take my breath away.

Cassie and her husband don't want to know the baby's gender, so I decided around month four to drop the phrase "him or her" and instead use "he" (even though "her" would be an equally fine thing). There's nothing scientific in my reasoning. This just feels like a "he" experience. Although, when I was pregnant with Carlene, I was convinced she was a boy and had a boy name picked out (Caleb Martin), only to hear the doctor announce, "It's a girl!" This time feels like a he, too, so he's probably a she.

Anyway, I first heard and felt his presence in May. The night before Cassie's obstetrician appointment, I stayed at her house, and the things grandparents tried to describe about the indescribable started to make sense. I was getting something out of the refrigerator when Cassie exclaimed, "Oooooh!" Her eyes were wide, and she laughed and put her hand on her lower right abdomen.

"Baby kicked and I saw it! Here, Mom, feel this!" I put my hand on the spot he'd kicked and held my breath. A few seconds later—pop! Grandbaby landed a punch in the dead center of my palm.

What an awe-filled space that is, feeling the life movements of a human being crawling around inside the very person who moved in me twenty-two years before. Not much astonishes me, but Grandbaby rendered me speechless. I had a pathetic lack of vocabulary at that moment, and could only describe that punch as "cool."

It got even better the next day when the doctor took out a Doppler and placed it on Cassie's belly. Within seconds, Grandbaby's heart whispered in the room, a soft pucker and unpucker, one hundred forty nine beats per minute. There was a moment of static and then the heartbeat sounded again.

"Did you hear that?" the doctor asked. My daughter was propped up on her elbows, her face with a smile I'd never seen before.

"Hear it? I felt it!" she laughed. The static had been the baby moving.

You could have told me the world was ending and it wouldn't have wiped the smile off my face. At that one moment, we were the universe. My daughter, her baby, and me aligned like the Earth, the moon, and the sun. It was one of those fleeting, perfect, indelible moments; the ones that, in remembering, comfort us during difficult moments.

When Cassie broke her hip in the Army Reserve, a doctor told her she might have problems during pregnancy. While you always hope this kind of prediction will be proven wrong, this one was spot on. Every night, Cassie struggles to find a comfortable position to sleep in. She told me this on the phone a while ago, but I had the sad opportunity to watch her and listen to her deal with the pain a few weeks ago.

The night before her baby shower, after washing my face and getting ready for bed, I walked past her room and heard her crying softly. I looked in and saw her hunched over the side of the bed, her hair falling around her face. Her husband was softly rubbing her back. I sat down next to her and put my arm around her shoulder. I've seen my children hurt, but never had I felt so impotent as a mother. Not a kiss, not a bandage, not all the money in the world could make her pain go away. And so we sat, and she cried, and the moment was what it was.

She says the baby is worth any amount of pain, and so I think about his whisper heartbeat, his kicking feet and punching fists, and imagine the time when he'll rest on Cassie's hip instead of stretching it from the inside.

As I wait for the baby to be born, I try to walk in that space between overbearing and never there. So far I'm doing a pretty good job, in my own humble judgement. I tolerate my son-in-law's grandmotherly nicknames, and I didn't camp out on their front steps to see the video of the ultrasound a few months ago. I was pretty sad, though, when I did see the photos from the ultrasound on their refrigerator and I didn't recognize anything. It was like looking at a 3-D puzzle. Only once Cassie pointed things out to me and I took a few steps back and shifted my eyes around and blurred them a little could I kind of make out a face, an eye, and an arm.

In two months (no less, I hope), I'll see his face, eyes, and arms in real life. My perfect moment grandbaby, the indescribable, the person who is already teaching me about the unexplainable feelings of grandparenthood.

Today's the Day!
Posted October 12, 2007

I'm blogging this morning from the hospital in Pittsburgh where Cassie is laying in a bed a few feet away from me, happy from an epidural. I'm so excited I could explode!

I got the warning call at 10:30 last night. Cassie's water broke. She said she'd call me from the hospital. I went back to bed, thinking about what I should wear. I fell asleep, kind of. Just enough to dream some really weird dreams. The phone rang a few hours later.

"It's baby time!" she said.

I packed a bag, called Carlene, and got in the Jeep. There were no cars on the road, and despite some rain and construction, I made great time. In exactly sixty-eight minutes, I was in Carlene's parking lot.

Now, six hours later, I'm tired. Carlene and I shared the couch while Matt tried to sleep in the chair. We all drifted a little, but mostly we laid awake and were quiet, listening to the baby's heartbeat on the monitor.

Matt just called Cassie a "little talk machine" because she and her nurse were chatting like old friends. I love that kid.

There are nurses everywhere in here now and Cassie wants to watch *Saved By the Bell*.

I love watching Matt love Cassie.

It's A... Claire!

Claire Raelyn is perfect! She was born at 12:02 p.m. She weighs six pounds, thirteen ounces, and is eighteen inches long. She has big dark eyes and black hair, her mother's long narrow feet and fingers and thick earlobes, and her father's nose. Her skin is porcelain pink and flawless, and she pooped three times the first hour of her life. Watching her birth and holding her for the first time changed me in ways I can't process yet. I love her so much.

And to think I almost missed it! Carlene and I had gone to the cafeteria around 11:15 to get lunch for us and for Matt after being assured nothing would happen before we got back. Thirty minutes later, as we walked back to her room, we saw a lot of activity, and I heard Cassie asking, "Where's my mom?" The doctor walked into the hallway, saw me, and told me I needed to get in there *now*!

I dropped my food in the waiting room across the hall and took my place on Cassie's right side near her head, supporting her as she pushed. Matt was in front of me holding up her right leg. As the baby's head crowned, he looked at me and asked, "Boy or girl?" I said, "It's a boy." He said "I think it's a boy, too." Cassie, annoyed with both of us, yelled with the final push, "It's a girl!"

And true enough, it was a girl.

I stood over my granddaughter's bassinette, so completely and utterly in awe as I watched her looking around and breathing, and I couldn't stop staring, smiling, crying, and saying, "Oh my god, she's perfect!"

Someone offered to take my picture. Then my daughter called to me from her bed. "Mom, her name is Claire Raelynn."

Are you kidding me?

My name is part of her name.

I drove home in stunned silence.

My world is completely different now.

I am a grandmother.

I Finally Feel like a Grandma. Or is it Grammy?
Posted October 2007

I'm learning that you don't magically transform from *not* being a grandma to being the kind of grandma you imagine you *should* be. It is taking a fair amount of patience and blind trust to know that what I've been feeling the past few weeks is OK.

I loved Claire before I met her, when she was more a thought than flesh, and I knew that the nature of this kind of "love-in-anticipation" is to change and grow. The larger my daughter's belly, the more complex my love for her and the growing baby. Yet reason flies out the window when bombarded with intense emotion.

The day Claire was born, I was tired and completely removed from any semblance of a comfort zone. Middle-of-the-night phone call, middle-of-the-night bag packing, middle-of-the-night drive to the hospital, middle-of-the-night seeing my daughter hooked up to monitors. Nothing felt real. Waiting for Claire was like standing at the arrival gate at the airport to greet a relative you've never met and hoped you'd recognize. All day I waited to feel like a grandma; to feel some distinct feeling that I would inherently recognize as grandparent love. But no fairy dust fell from the sky. When Claire was born, I was overwhelmed with awe that the little baby I'd known as a mere thought had come out with toes and fingers, big eyes, and a little hair. So much emotion had entered the room at once that it was like grabbing Jell-O. I couldn't clutch one feeling to experience fully.

Some people process their emotions immediately. I can't. I don't trust those first feelings. I need to step back and examine the details; run them through my mind a few times before I let them sink in.

I saw Claire for a while after she was born and again the next day. I went to stay with Cassie and Matt and Claire for a few days when they got home, and I didn't understand why a distinct "grandma" feel hadn't yet settled in. What I felt was fear. I was afraid of taking over, of offering advice, of being a pain-in-the-ass, of being in the way. The space was all so unfamiliar. I was afraid I'd love Claire too much. I was afraid she'd go away. I was afraid I'd fail.

When I went home and I was surrounded by familiar things, I began to realize that what I felt for Claire was unique to me. The more I thought about Claire, the more my own "grandma feel" emerged, like an early spring crocus out of the snow. I found that plain on which to move around as the grandma I'm meant to be. I found a place of peace that allows me to feel everything I need to feel and not be afraid.

My husband and I went to see Claire yesterday, and I was completely comfortable with my new-found grandma feelings. I held her with confidence and was no longer fearful of her tiny body.

I am not like any other grandparent. No grandparent is.

Claire seems very alert and wiggly for an eight-day-old, or perhaps I'm just forgetting how eight-day-olds behave. I swore she was going to push herself on to the floor today the way her legs dug into my stomach when I was holding her in my lap. Her arms flail and her head moves from side to side. She was fascinated with Grandpa Larry's brown shirt. She stared at it for several minutes. I took videos and photos, laughed with my daughters, and teased my son-in-law. This is our new normal with a new member on our family team.

These new feelings make sense. They aren't what I expected, but then, how boring would life be if we knew ahead of time what every life moment would feel like? All I have to do now is figure out my grandparent name. Grandma? Granny? Grammy? Mimi? I'm leaning toward Grammy. Grammy Lynn. Yeah. I like it. Grammy Lynn.

Once a Mother, Always a Mother
Posted October 2007

My daughter and her husband have this whole new baby thing under control. Nursing? No problem. Claire gained a pound her first week home. Nights? Piece of cake. Claire sleeps in three- to four-hour intervals. A little projectile vomit, some outrageous poops? No problem. The dresser is filled with many bibs and onesies and sleepers.

There's no real exhaustion in this house.

So why am I here in such a perfectly functioning house?

To mother the mother.

In the months I spent anticipating what it would be like to be a grandmother, part of me anticipated a shift in my usefulness as Cassie's mother. I thought, wrongly, that maybe my job as her mom would be done when she became a mother because we would all now focus on the baby.

But that's not how motherhood works. Once a mother, always a mother, and just like relationships of every kind, the mother-child relationship is always changing and adapting. Cassie had a baby *and* she's still my daughter. My presence in this seemingly perfectly functioning house is comforting to her.

I cook a little, hold the baby while Cass takes a shower, do the laundry, and watch *Gilmore Girls* with her as she nurses. We talk the same, behave the same toward each other, and love each other as we always have. We just have a new girl in our inner circle.

It's now 8:30 in the evening. Matt is sitting on the couch, legs outstretched on the cushions. Claire is snuggled in the crook of his arm and sound asleep. Cassie is sleeping with her head on his left leg. The Pittsburgh Penguins are playing the Toronto Maple Leafs. I'm plugged into iTunes and writing. Love permeates the room and there's nothing mysterious about it. It just is. Mother to daughter. Husband to wife. Parent to child.

Grammy Nanny
Posted January 2008

5:45 a.m.

"Mom?" My daughter gently shakes me awake. "Mom, just wanted you to get your bearings. I'm going to work soon."

It's Wednesday. I'm in Pittsburgh. These details thaw slowly as the dream I was just having about dogs and preachers and Hillary Clinton fades. My stomach tightens a bit. I went to bed last night apprehensive about today. I agreed months ago to watch my granddaughter all day on Wednesdays and on Thursday mornings when Cassie went back to work, but talking about it is different than actually doing it.

I kick back the covers and turn on a light.

6:30 a.m.

Final instructions. Claire's in my room lying on a big round pillow on the floor with her pink elephant friend, Ellie, next to her. She's looking at me as I type. Staring actually, like she knows I'm a little concerned about this nanny gig. We both have a lot to learn today. I've not spent twelve hours alone with a three-month-old since Cassie was three months old, twenty-three years ago.

Big yawn (her, not me). Maybe we'll both get a nap soon.

6:40 a.m.

Claire kicks and talks and squeals in a high-pitched sing-song voice. She's like her mother in so many ways. Already she seems to want to be older than she is. Claire was born a week early and has been holding her head up from the very beginning, unsteady at first, but now she lies on her stomach and holds her head up, looking around the room, drooling on her blanket. Sometimes she'll flip over to her back and wonder how the heck she did that.

The drool is immense some days. So is the fist-sucking. She has two small bumps on her bottom gums. Soon she'll cut her first teeth. Claire is in the middle between those babies who, on average, cut their bottom teeth between four and seven months, and the one in two thousand who are actually born with teeth. She's considered young for teeth, but she's not considered odd, either.

6:55 a.m.

Claire's on my bed with me helping me write. She sucks in her bottom lip and flattens her mouth. She looks like my mother when she'd take out her dentures and smile at my kids. They'd scream in delight and beg her to do it again and again.

Another big yawn and a frustrating little cry. My writing is boring her. She's not the first person I've bored, I'm sure.

7:20 a.m.

Crisis! We have bottles but no nipples. I search the kitchen to no avail. Before he left for work, Matt said to call him and not Cassie if I had any questions because he does twelve-hour Claire duty on Sundays and knows how hard it is to convince Claire that we're almost as good as Mommy when we know deep down we're not. I call his cell phone.

"Matt! Where are the nipples?" (Not a conversation most mothers-in-law have with their sons-in-law.)

"Damn. I'm sorry, I was going to tell you that before I left and totally forgot."

Two minutes later, I found the nipples and heated up my first bottle as Grammy Nanny.

7:26 a.m.

Peace has returned to the house.

8:12 a.m.

No sleeping yet. Claire is lying against my chest, face out, as I type. She's watching the screen intently. I lean over and kiss her head. Babies heads are mesmerizing. Soft and fuzzy, and they smell good (most of the time). Her head feels nice pressed against my lips. So calming and centering.

Sadie the dog is sleeping on the floor. Classical music is playing in Claire's room.

Uh oh. Major noises from down under. Thank god for "unbeatable leakage protection." We're heading to the changing table.

8:21 a.m.

Claire is in her crib listening to Bach and watching her mobile spin slowly. She's talking to the panda moving above her.

9:00 a.m.

Claire falls asleep. I lay her on pillows on the couch and slip in a "Walk Away the Pounds" video.

9:15 a.m.

Claire wakes up. I pause the video, put her in her vibrating chair, hand her a toy and turn the video back on. She seems amused watching me do kicks and knee lifts and sidesteps and kickbacks. She plays long enough for me to do two of the three miles. Not much of a workout, but at least it's something.

9:47 a.m.

I need breakfast. I put Claire on the changing table of her Pack 'n Play. She's talking to the bears on the mobile and trying to touch them. I can see her from the kitchen as I make an omelet.

10:10 a.m.

Perfect timing. My omelet is on a plate on a table near the couch. Claire is mad at the mobile bears, so I prop her up next to me on the couch. She's sitting like a big girl, staring at something by her feet. I don't see anything particularly interesting, but then, I'm not three months old. She's seeing things for the first time. It's kind of sad that I routinely miss the interesting things right in front of me.

10:23 a.m.
Another concentrated look on Claire's face. Another rumble down below. Back we go to the changing table.

11:07 a.m.
Ah, blessed sleep (the baby, not me). Her sleep time is my work time. I don't know how much time I've got, so I'd better take advantage of every minute.

11:45 a.m.
Work time's over, I think. I peek over at Claire lying on the couch. She's shifting positions. Her eyes are half committed to waking. Is she going back to sleep? Yes, I think she is. Shhhhh…. Please God, don't send a UPS driver to our door.

11:50 a.m.
Another rumble down under. This one has seeped up the front of her onesie. Claire is wide awake. I would be, too, if I did that in my pants.

12:25 p.m.
Claire drank a bottle and is still saying no to sleep. Again, she's just like her mother. As a baby, Cassie was always too busy to sleep. There was too much to see and do. Claire just wants to kick around on the couch and talk to me and the pillow and her green and purple fuzzy blanket. And her fist.

I've survived the first six hours. Only six more until Daddy gets home. I see heavy eyes over on the couch. I think Claire needs a nap. I *need* her to need a nap. But I'm living by Claire's agenda today. Whatever she wants, she gets. If she wants a nap, great. If not, that's OK, too. It has to be. She's Claire and she's calling the shots.

Auntie Carly
Posted May 2008

I take a lot of photos of my granddaughter, but some moments should be preserved in words and memory only.

This afternoon, I heard Claire fussing just twenty-five minutes into her nap. I was in the guest room writing, but I knew her auntie would tend to her. An hour later, I checked to see where they were. I found Carlene asleep in the rocking chair in the nursery as Claire lay asleep in her arms, wrapped in her fuzzy green blanket, her head resting in the crook of Carlene's left arm. It was a perfect moment of peace and stillness, and most of all, love.

When I write about Claire, I often mention her mother or her father, but Auntie Carly is probably the third most important person in Claire's life. It's been interesting watching my oldest daughter interact with her niece these past seven months. Carlene is not one for public displays of affection, but that ideology flies out the window when Claire is around. She puts seasoned baby-talkers, neck-kissers, and peek-a-booers like me to shame.

Carlene has always been forthcoming about her feelings for Cassie and me. The three of us are a tight little enclave, and we trust each other implicitly. She loves her grandparents and aunts and uncles, but she's not as publicly gushy with her love for them as she is with Cassie and me. She's not stoic, but she's a lot like her father, even though he died when she was a baby. She's as much a product of nature as she is nurture.

One way you can really tell Carlene loves her niece is her tolerance of Claire's bodily functions. Carlene detests puke, snot, pee, and poop. When she was little and had the stomach flu, she willed herself not to throw up. She also refused to cough a good hard get-up-the-phlegm cough when she had a cold. I'd beg her to cough and she'd simply say no. And getting her potty trained, well, that's another story and one I'll never tell because she'd never speak to me again.

Carlene is more than I felt I ever deserved, and watching her today with her niece in her arms, so soft and tender, I thanked God I did something in my life to warrant such a moment as that.

With my apologies to the Apostle Paul, I've rewritten his famous passage on love from his first letter to the Corinthians because, to me, Carlene is the embodiment of how he describes love: Carlene is patient. Carlene is kind. She (usually) does not envy and she almost never boasts. Carlene is proud in the right way. She's not rude, except maybe on a really bad PMS day, but she always apologizes. She is not self-seeking, it takes a lot to get her angry, and she's never thrown something I've done wrong back in my face. Carlene does not delight in evil, but rejoices in the truth. Carlene always protects, always trusts, always hopes, always perseveres. Carlene's love never fails.

It's Your Second Birthday ... Already?
Posted October 2009

Happy second birthday, sweet Claire! Even though tomorrow is your birthday, your party is today. Your mom bought you a Hello Kitty cake and I made spaghetti sauce so your dad could make meatball tortellini.

We're not sure we'll sing the birthday song to you when you blow out your candles. You're not one for clapping and cheering crowds.

When your mom cut her long hair to donate it to Locks of Love this year, the women in the salon clapped and you started to cry.

You can say a lot of words, but you don't have a name for me yet. You call both Grandpa Larry and Grandpa Frank "Papa" and Carlene "Auntie," but when someone shows you a photo of me and they say, "Who's that?" you just laugh. Or if I show you the photo and say, "Who's that?" you throw your arms around me. That's better than any name, of course, but I still wonder what you'll call me in the coming year.

You call yourself "You Me." I can see how you would. When you see a photo of yourself and we ask, "Who's that?" you say, "Me!" and we say, "Right! That's you!" Therefore, you call yourself "You Me."

In August, we had our first sleepover at my house. You love the back yard and the wood duck with the loose head in Grandpa's office and the red toy tractor and the big stems of fake flowers that you take around the house making everyone smell. We go to the library where you love to play with the big table of blocks and the "choo-choos."

Your favorite song is "The Hot Dog Song" by Mickey Mouse. I don't know how many times I've played it for you. Once, when Luca was crying and your mom had to take care of him, she called me and put you on the phone so we could talk while she put him to bed. I played that song on my computer and held the receiver to the speakers. I knew you were dancing because I heard the phone bumping around. Then you'd yell, "Hot dog!" and I'd play it again.

One of the best toys I gave you this year didn't cost a thing: your turtle sand box. A neighbor gave it to me because his daughters had outgrown it. The weekend Luca was born, I bought sand and filled it up and you played in it for hours. That was the weekend I bought your tricycle, too. Such a big girl you are! Your old Grammy gets a little teary when she thinks of you growing up so fast.

Sometimes, when I put you down to bed and we're lying there in the dark, I think of how much I love you and how thankful I am you were born. I don't say anything out loud, but it's like you read my mind because you take your pacifier out of your mouth and say "Yeah" and then pop it back in and continue sucking on it and rubbing your blanket.

I can't wait to see what your third year on this earth has in store for you and for us. We'll bake Christmas cookies in a few months, and I'll show you how to make pine cone bird feeders next summer. By the way, you call birds "bees." In fact, anything that flies is a "bee" right now.

When I was a little girl, a singer named Gilbert O'Sullivan recorded a song called "Clair." Even though I was young, I understood the love he was describing and hoped one day to love someone like that. I had no idea it would be you and that you'd be a Claire, too! Here are some of the lyrics:

> *Clair, the moment I met you I swear*
> *I felt as if something somewhere*
> *Had happened to me, which I couldn't see*
> *But try as hard as I might, I don't know why*
> *You get to me in a way I can't describe*
> *Words mean so little when you look up and smile*

This song still makes me cry. Happy tears, of course, and you probably think Grammy's too emotional and it's OK to roll your eyes, but I love you and I hope I let you know that in everything I say and do.

Update: A month after her birthday, Claire was staying overnight at my house, and after I read her a book, I tucked her in bed and sang "Twinkle, Twinkle Little Star," because she won't go to sleep otherwise. When I finished, she took out her pacifier and said, "I love you, Rammy!"

At last, I had a name.

Lynn Haraldson

The Walk
Posted March 2010

I used to think walking was merely a way to get from point A to point B or a means of exercise. Sometimes both. A walk is a walk is a walk…until I walked with Claire.

The girl doesn't know it, but she always knows exactly what to do and say to put things in perspective.

This morning during breakfast, we decided to walk uptown to the post office and library. She put on her Dora sneakers and tan jacket, and I surprised her with new purple mittens with hearts and rainbows that I bought her on winter clearance. This made her very happy.

I put on my backpack loaded with the envelopes that needed to be mailed, my phone, and some money since I was pretty sure I had library fines. Claire put on her Dora backpack and off we went.

The weather was lovely, sunny and about forty degrees. Since sidewalks are inconsistent for the first few blocks, we cut down an alley to avoid street traffic. As we passed a garage, Claire asked, "Where'd my shadow go?"

"What, honey?" I asked.

She stopped. "My shadow, Rammy."

Shadow? But of course! I hadn't thought about my shadow since I was a kid.

"It's hidden by the garage," I told her. "Let's move back into the sunshine."

"There it is! It's big!" she said. "You have a big shadow, too, Rammy!" She waved. "See my hand?"

I waved back with both hands. She giggled.

"I see your fingers in the shadow," she said.

When we turned the corner we were back on a sidewalk and our shadows were in front of us. Claire hopped over each crack for the rest of the block, thrilled that her shadow kept up with her.

We got to a corner and had to cross a street. I was holding her hand and was just going to walk her across when it dawned on me that I could teach her how to properly cross a street.

"Always stop before walking out on to the street," I said. "Look to your left. Do you see a car coming?"

Looking very concentrated, Claire peered down the street. "No," she said seriously.

"Now look to your right. Any cars?"

"Nope."

"OK, that means we can cross safely."

We walked down a street I've walked for years, but I'd never noticed that the old Victorian house on Seventh Avenue was blue or that the rental next door had green trim until Claire pointed it out. Then she spied tiny purple flowers in the next yard.

"Those are crocuses," I told her.

"Crocheches," she repeated. Close enough.

I wouldn't have noticed them on an ordinary walk. I see them in my own yard because I'm looking for them after a long winter, but crocuses are even better when you're not seeking them out, and they're spectacular when you unexpectedly get to introduce them to a two-year-old who loves the colors purple and green.

"I run real fast, Rammy!" and she took off. I kept up by walking more briskly, but it was fun to let her get to the next house a little before I did.

We were getting close to another corner and she took my hand. We stopped, she looked both ways.

"No cars," she said, and led me safely to the other side.

We went to the post office first, which is next to the library. I handed the envelopes to the mail clerk.

Claire pulled on my jeans. "I wanna see." I lifted her up to sit on the counter.

"I like your mittens," said the clerk. Saying nothing, Claire smiled and looked down at the hearts and rainbows.

"Can she have a lollipop?" he whispered to me. I nodded.

"Would you like a lollipop?" he asked.

"Yes," she said boldly.

From under the counter, he took out a brown grocery bag. Claire reached in and pulled out a small chocolate flavored Tootsie-Pop. She's definitely my granddaughter.

"What do you say?" I whispered.

"Thank you," she said quietly, staring again at her mittens, but he heard her.

"You're welcome!"

Claire insisted I open the wrapper before we left the post office. I didn't want her to bring it into the library, so we sat on a bench out front and she ate her lollipop.

"A black truck," she pointed to the street. "That's Papa's truck." Her dad's father is "Papa" and he drives a pickup.

"No, that's not Papa's truck, but it looks like it," I said.

"That's a red car," she continued and crunched her lollipop.

"Hear that?" she asked.

"That's a blue jay," I said.

"Blue jay," she repeated and took another bite of her lollipop.

After the library, we walked home in similar fashion. Birds. Cars. Flowers. Cracks in the sidewalk. Watching Claire observe the world around her, the world I've very much taken for granted, I felt a profound sense of belonging. I have a shadow. I know love. Oh that the world could feel such peace.

Common Ground

They'll All Fit
Posted February 2013

Grandbaby number four will be here sometime in the next few, several, maybe ten days, so my phone is never off and always charged.

You'd think I'd be used to it by now. Cassie has had three fairly easy pregnancies and deliveries, but it's still difficult to accept that there's not one thing I can do to guarantee she and the baby will be fine.

And as if worry wasn't enough, self-doubt has joined the fun. I keep asking myself, do I have what it takes to be a good grandmother to four children? (Heck, I'll settle for marginally competent!) I've eaten my way through that question more than a few times this week and, as you can guess, I got no answer. Turns out, I was asking the right question of the wrong person.

Last night I took Claire to her taekwondo class. On the ride there, she talked about who will be at her house to take care of her when her mommy is having the baby. She rattled off a list of people she wants around her: me, Papa Larry, Grandma Julia, Papa Frank, Auntie Carly and Uncle Ben. She wants to sleep in her bed tent and wants Luca, who will soon be four, to sleep in her secret hiding place, aka, her closet, which has a sheer curtain for a door and lots of pillows inside. She didn't mention two-year-old Mae. Luca is her best friend. Mae is someone Claire tolerates.

She was talking faster than usual, and I realized she was seeking reassurance that everything will be OK, that if she woke up one morning and her mommy and daddy weren't there, that she would not be alone. And there was my answer: I know how to do that! I know how to make Claire feel safe. I've been doing it for more than five years!

With my new-found courage, I went to Cassie's this morning to watch the kids so she could go to her doctor's appointment in peace. I sat on the couch and all three grabbed their blankies and snuggled up around me. I remembered what I told Claire before Mae was born, that I'd have to grow a third leg so I could fit another baby on my lap. Over the next year, every time she saw me, she asked me about that third leg. I asked Cassie how I'd possibly have room for a fourth baby and she said, "You have long arms. They'll all fit."

Audrey Rose
Posted February 2013

I got the call at 7:30 last night. Water broke, bags are packed, it's baby time.

The kids were still awake when I got there, and their nervous excitement was palpable. Cassie and Matt left at 8:15 and the kids waved goodbye from the front window. We talked and read books, and by 9:30, they were sound asleep.

Cassie texted me throughout the night with updates. Two centimeters at 2:30, five at 5, seven at 6.

"My epidural wore off on the left side. I can't believe you went natural with us. Shit hurts man," she texted at 6:15. I replied, "I had no choice."

A few minutes later: "Will be pushing in about 10-15 min. 8 cm."

I knew the next half hour in Cassie's world would be beautifully chaotic with pushing and panting, doctor's commands, blood, pain, and sweat. I watched her birth Claire, so I know she births babies with determination and grace. I also knew my son-in-law was giving her one hundred ten percent. I got dressed and went downstairs. In the quiet kitchen, I played Words with Friends, ate a banana, and thought for sure Cassie was birthing a boy.

Claire woke up and came downstairs. She got up on to the stool next to mine and asked, "What is it? What's the baby? A boy or girl?"

I told her I didn't know yet. She asked for a banana and she showed me how she peels them.

At 7:15, my son-in-law sent the first photo of the baby: "It's Audrey Rose! 6 lbs 14 oz!"

"You have a sister!" I told Claire and showed her the photo.

"Ohhhh! She's so cuuuute! It's a really, really pretty name!"

I texted and called family and friends as Claire typed the alphabet on my computer.

"Why are people so excited?" Claire asked, as my phone dinged and rang.

"Because so many people want to know who Audrey is," I said.

"Oh," she said, and kept typing.

I heard Luca walk into the bathroom. Claire went upstairs and said, "You were right! We have a sister! Her name is Audrey Rose!"

"Awwwww...that's so cuuuute!" said Luca, flushing the toilet.

"Wash your hands!" I yelled up the stairs.

"I did!" he said.

"Dude, there's no way you washed your hands yet. Wash them!" I said. The water turned on.

Luca came down and sat on my lap as I continued texting friends and family. He typed his own line on my computer: jhzg4etreegrfetsgqwhewfhtrthygtyhy56htre, naming each letter and number as he typed.

Matt sent me another photo of Audrey and I showed the kids.

"Are we gonna have *that* baby?" Luca asked. Yes, I said, that's the one who's going to live in your house for the next eighteen years, at least.

Mae woke up at 8:15. I went upstairs and changed her diaper and brought her downstairs. I showed her the photos of Audrey.

"Mommy's baby," she said over and over.

"Yes, that's Mommy's baby. Her name is Audrey." Mae insisted I keep Audrey's photo on my computer screen. If I responded to something on Facebook, she'd say, "See Mommy's baby!" and I'd have to bring the photo back on the screen. Like Luca, I don't think she fully understands that "Mommy's baby" is coming home to stay on Thursday.

I sent one last text to my son-in-law before getting the kids ready to bring them to the hospital.

"Thank you for Audrey."

"Hey, thanks for Cassie," he wrote back. "She's just an awesome woman."

Indeed.

5. Weight Part 1 — The Greatest Hits

"Her fifteen minutes went by so fast."

— Don Henley

It started simply enough. On New Year's Day 2005, I — like millions of other people — resolved to lose weight. And I did.

In April 2007, a friend told me *Oprah* was looking for people who had lost one hundred pounds or more through diet and exercise to be guests on an upcoming show. I met that criteria, but I hadn't considered sharing my weight loss with anyone outside my friends, family, and the handful of people I knew online through Weight Watchers' discussion boards or my blog. After a few days (and a few glasses of wine), I wrote a letter, selected some photos, dropped the envelope in the mail, and forgot about it.

Four months later, I came home from a hike and there was a message on my answering machine from Harpo Studios. The nervous excitement I felt in that moment was the first of many such moments over the next five months.

In addition to *Oprah*, I said yes to *People* magazine, *Today*,

Entertainment Tonight, CNN, the local news, two national radio shows, and a magazine in New Zealand. I said no to *The Tyra Show* (I promised I'd babysit my granddaughter) and *Weight Watchers Magazine* (I was exhausted), and was not selected to be on *Ellen* because I'd been on *Oprah*.

Being in the spotlight was my choice; no one held my feet over fire. But the spotlight burned bright, literally and figuratively. My image started showing up online in advertisements for bogus weight-loss products. I was getting mail at home from "fans" seeking everything from my autograph to absolution. A British tabloid asked if I had loose skin and offered to pay me for photos. I felt I'd lost control of my message, so I declined requests for further interviews and returned to the medium in which I was most comfortable and could retain the most control of my words, image, and integrity: blogging.

For this chapter, I selected writing that represents my experience before the spotlight, my experiences in the spotlight, and what I learned from the spotlight.

One Thing

While I journaled and thought long and hard about why I wanted to lose weight this last time, the one thing that put me on this journey was a photograph from the night of my daughter's twentieth birthday, December 12, 2004.

I'd offered to cook Cassie one of her favorite meals, but she insisted we go out.

"It's snowing," I said.

"Mom…," she said, like a finger snap.

"Fine," I sighed.

There was no use arguing with her. It was only flurries, and she'd just take out the guilt card and make me feel even worse. I pulled my hair back in a ponytail like I always did. My haircut was uneven and the color was a combination of store-bought dye, dark roots, and strands of gray. I'd stopped going to the salon because the chair was as uncomfortable as staring at my reflection in the mirror. I trimmed my bangs when the hair grew past my eyes, and I lopped off the ends when they looked frayed. I bought a bottle of color every few months when the gray made me as depressed as my weight.

I pulled a stretchy red sweater over my stretchy black pants with the small hole and a permanent stain on the leg. Not much fit anymore and I didn't have the money to upgrade my wardrobe another size. I had garbage bags full of clothes in every size from 16 to 28, but what fit now was 30/32 and I only had a few shirts and pants that size. I threw on some socks and boots but no jewelry. My goal was always to remain as unnoticed as possible.

"You look nice," said my husband, as he put on his winter coat.

"Whatever," I said.

We met Cassie and my other daughter Carlene at the restaurant, and despite the weather, the place was filled with pre-holiday parties. Most of the diners didn't notice I was there, but I imagined that as I walked in everyone thought, 'Oh my, she's big.' And probably a few did. We were seated next to a window with a view of the snow falling on the Allegheny River and I eased into a chair, red-faced from the short walk from the parking lot.

The girls were animated, as usual, talking over each other and carrying on two conversations at once. I knew it was futile to say no to a photo when Cassie handed her camera to Larry and said, "Take a picture of me and Mom!"

"Smile," he said, and I did.

"That's a nice photo of us, Mom," said Cassie as she scrolled through the photos.

"Yes, honey, it is," I lied.

At first glance I thought, 'How could you let yourself get that big?' Then something caught my eye. Cassie had placed her cheek next to mine and she was beaming. She was happy because she was with her mother on her birthday. Not her morbidly obese mother, her ill-dressed mother, her isolated, guarded, self-loathing mother—those were my descriptors. Cassie loved me just the way I was.

I had allowed weight to become my essence. I let it dress me and define me and gauge my self-worth. That photo of Cassie and me challenged me to see and feel the three-hundred-plus-pound body in which I lived and to decide if I was going to allow my weight to be my personal judge and jury.

Who's That Girl?
Posted November 2006

I was in Arkansas last week visiting my Aunt Shirley, whom I hadn't seen since October 2004. I've lost a lot of weight since then, and I'm still trying to wrap my brain around my before and current photos.

There aren't many before photos of me, at least at my heaviest, which was between three hundred and three hundred fifteen pounds. I don't know an exact number because other than going to the doctor, I stopped weighing myself after two hundred twenty pounds. I was pretty successful at avoiding cameras whenever possible, but I'm beginning to think maybe that wasn't such a good thing. By avoiding cameras I was also avoiding the truth. What I saw in the mirror was what I chose to see.

The woman I was in the before photo is physically a stranger to me, but I know everything she was thinking and feeling in that moment: She did *not* want a photo taken. It was bad enough that my back was killing me after standing for an hour rolling lefse dough. I knew, but refused to admit, that my back hurt because I was morbidly obese. Instead I blamed heredity. My Dad has a bad back so naturally I did, too.

I knew my weight was a topic of conversation between my mother and Shirley; not in a mean-spirited way, but physical appearance is important in my family, at least to the generations before me. I've been told all my life, "You're such a pretty girl…if only you lost some weight."

Even typing that made me roll my eyes.

Now, one hundred forty-six pounds lighter, I am almost half the physical person I was in October 2004. Problems solved, right? If only.

My head hasn't caught up to my body. When I look at that photo of me from last week and compare it to the me from before, I feel defensive. I want to protect the former me from the me now. It's like I've become the people I tried to avoid when I was fat. I don't know if "forgiven" is the right word, but I've accepted the fat me, the person who struggled with hypothyroidism and depression which led to a huge weight gain. I am gentle with her and understand her a lot more than I understand this thinner chick who wants to forget the fat chick.

It's a startling comparison photo. I have it posted on my weight loss website to serve as an inspiration to people struggling with their weight, that with hard work and perseverance, it can be done. But despite my smiling face, getting thinner is a much bigger struggle emotionally than I ever imagined it would be.

Oprah (2007)
Posted Sunday, November 4

It hasn't hit me yet that in a few days I will meet Oprah. I'm so busy packing and organizing for my trip to Chicago that I've not had time for it to sink in.

I was selected to be a guest on *Oprah* after writing a letter in April, sharing my weight-loss story and some photos. I forgot about the letter until one day in August, a screener at Harpo Studios left a message on our answering machine. "Would you mind giving me a call back?" she said. Mind? Isn't there some kind of law that if Oprah calls, you call back?

Shari, who suggested I write the letter in the first place, is booked on the same flight. I don't think I could do this without her. I haven't flown in ten years, so I'm a little nervous about that, too, but that's why they invented Xanax, and Shari is crazy excited and in her energy I find strength.

Monday, November 5

I'm tired. Wait, I take that back. I'm exhausted. I'm also homesick and a little sad, and because of why I'm in Chicago, I've got a lot of self-doubt going on. I want to go home, forget all this, and crawl into my own bed.

This morning, I met Shari at my daughter's house in Pittsburgh on the way to the airport. I held my granddaughter for a while, changed her diaper, gave her a little kiss on her fuzzy head and we headed to the airport. Except for a little turbulence, it was a smooth ride to Chicago. A driver loaded us and our luggage into a black stretch limousine and took us to Harpo Studios.

I was fine when I got there. Everyone was nice. I met my producer and waited in a room filled with apples and bananas and granola bars. One of the production assistants said they usually keep the room stocked with bagels and cream-filled croissants, but they thought since they were producing a weight-loss show, they should offer healthier fare. I said they should do that all the time. He just laughed.

Also in the waiting room were a few of the other people who will be on the show. One has lost three hundred fifty pounds and the other more than four hundred. I wondered how my measly one-hundred-sixty-five-pound loss measured up to that kind of tenacity. My story suddenly felt insignificant, and I'm afraid I brought that feeling into the audio room. During the recording, I spoke in a quiet voice. That strong me in the video they asked me to send during the selection process last week was nowhere to be found.

I was instructed to answer carefully worded questions in full sentences. I had a microphone clipped to my sweater, a single bright light to my left, and a camera focused on me while a woman I'd never talked to before asked me questions about what and how I felt emotionally and physically when I was morbidly obese. I struggled to stay focused, and inside I was crashing and burning.

The thirty minutes of audio will be edited to forty seconds, but I walked away feeling I hadn't conveyed my true feelings and that the audio guys will be lucky to come up with even a few seconds of usable material. I'll sound like an idiot on national television while photo after photo of me at my heaviest flashes across the monitor. What the hell was I thinking when I wrote that letter in April?

I realize I'm tired and so my feelings are magnified. I have to trust that tomorrow will be what tomorrow will be. Tonight, I'm in a lovely hotel in downtown Chicago. Tomorrow morning I will work out, eat breakfast, and walk along the Magnificent Mile. After lunch, a car will pick me up and take me to Macy's to shop for the clothes I will wear at the taping. I will remember to enjoy myself.

This isn't how I thought I'd feel tonight. This isn't the blog I thought I'd write. But I'm not as sad anymore having written it down, and my self-doubt has eased a bit. I'm still a little homesick, though.

Lynn Haraldson

Tuesday, November 6

Morning

I knew that a good night's sleep, a little Xanax, and some deep breathing, I would feel better. It helps to have a friend along, too. Shari and I dissected yesterday's events and concluded that it really wasn't as bad as it seemed. It was just overwhelming and unusual. Not a typical day in my life.

The weatherman said the winds will gust to forty mph today. This city's already a wind tunnel. What will forty mph feel like? I don't think I brought along enough hairspray.

Evening

Getting fitted for a bra is like wiggling yourself head first through a child's padded wire playground tunnel. I had so many women stuffing my breasts through straps and lace today that it might have qualified as foreplay.

Trying on clothes for four hours is hard work. I'd never taken my clothes on and off so many times, and never have I unabashedly undressed in front of a man I hadn't planned to sleep with. Michael is the head stylist for our show, and it was a matter of efficiency. No time for modesty. If I'd kicked him out every time I needed to take off one pair of jeans and put on another, we'd still be there.

Each of the twenty-one guests for this show needed three outfits for the Harpo folks to choose from. I ended up being photographed in six for some reason. They told Michael they wanted me in something tight, and tight is what he gave them. Tight jeans, tight dresses, tight tights. I have no idea which outfit they'll select (I'll find out in the morning), but I'm hoping for the purple knit dress and knee boots because we get to keep the outfit they choose and the dress is something I'd wear in real life. The other clothes I tried on today are way out of my league.

Tomorrow's schedule is packed. We'll start out at Harpo for a fitting and then we will go to a salon for a makeover. Afterwards, it's back to Harpo for rehearsal. I will not meet Oprah until Thursday when I walk out on stage. She doesn't like to meet guests, even celebrities, before taping. It takes away from the spontaneity of the conversation, she says. I haven't had time to be nervous about that. Give me time, though. It will happen.

Oh, and I talked to a few of the women who will be on the show and they all said the same thing about their audio taping experience yesterday. I was so relieved. I thought I was the only one.

Today was everything yesterday wasn't. I'm finally having…fun.

Thursday, November 8

Morning

Before rehearsal yesterday, there was an Oprah sighting while I was in the makeup chair. She was on her way to the studio to do a show with one hundred Osmonds. You know, Donny, Marie, and the rest. I briefly met Jimmy Osmond. He looks the same as he did when he was a kid. Nice guy, too.

The Harpo powers didn't pick the purple dress. They said they want me to be their "rocker chick." Me, a forty-four-year-old grandmother. They selected black skinny jeans and an off-the-shoulder clingy black shirt. Michael also picked out a big studded belt that costs more than my entire wardrobe at home, and knee-high suede boots. My (new) lacy bra straps will show, which feels really awkward because my mother always told me to never show your bra strap in public. Sorry, Mom.

After my hair and makeup were finished, I went to the bathroom. It was wall-to-wall Osmonds. When I finally made my way to the sink, I didn't recognize myself in the mirror. I was shocked, actually.

The reflection in the mirror was pretty, but it wasn't me. My hair was blown straight and flat ironed, and up close, the makeup made me look like a cadaver. Before going to bed last night, I couldn't get the mascara off my eyes, and my eyeballs were glued to the insides of my eyelids this morning. I'm definitely stopping at Walgreens when I get back to Pennsylvania later today and buy a bottle of makeup remover.

I'll write again after I get home and am in comfy clothes and my face is breathing again.

November 10

Two days ago, I was glammed up and shaking Oprah Winfrey's hand. Today, I'm wearing leggings and a sweater, and I've already been grocery shopping. It feels good to be home.

Here's the recap:

Shari and I packed our bags and went to the lobby to wait for the cars that would take us and the others to Harpo. It was like the last day of summer camp when everyone stands around talking, exchanging email addresses, and taking photos. The cars were an hour late, which turned out to be a good thing because it gave us all more time to calm our nerves.

At Harpo, the producers were in full "show mode." I was led right to the makeup chairs and afterwards, was handed off to the hair stylist. When that was done, a few of us had a final rehearsal. There were a lot more people in the studio than the day before. Camera people, sound people, and directors everywhere. My nerves were kicking in. We weren't allowed to bring any personal items into the studio after we arrived, but I had tucked a Xanax in my shoe, just in case.

After rehearsal, I went to the changing room where Michael helped me get dressed, then my producer went over the script with me, such as it was. It was a list of possible questions Oprah might ask, but, said the producer, she might ask something completely different and

in that case, I'd be on my own. Great. I could barely remember my name at that point.

We were taping the show at 1:30. At 12:45, four of us were called back to the stage. The director had made a change. We weren't going to walk out and sit between Bob Greene and Oprah as we'd rehearsed. He decided it would be better if we stood. Kelly was thrilled because she was sewn into a little green dress that had the possibility of showing the world a little too much Kelly if she was sitting. I worried because I didn't know what to do with my hands. I'm a hand talker, especially when I'm nervous. At least when I'm sitting I can fold them in my lap.

After showing us our new marks, we were whisked off stage because the audience was starting to file in. An audio person came over and hooked up a microphone to my bra, snaking it under my arm and through the top of my shirt. I did a quick sound check and she left me to hook up another guest.

1:15. Time to get lined up in the hallway outside the back of the studio. Hair and makeup people walked back and forth, fussing with our faces and hair. A producer said, "Oprah's walking," and we were led to another part of the hall so she wouldn't see us.

We watched the show on monitors. Nancy, who'd lost the most weight, was first. Then David, who once weighed six hundred fifty pounds. David's story made me well up with tears. The makeup artist saw me and whispered, "You can't cry!" So I paced the floor and blocked out David's voice.

After David, a producer took Kelly and me backstage. I was nervous, but not overwhelmingly. I'd adopted a "What's the worst that could happen?" approach. I fall? I lose my voice? I throw up? My producer told me to stand tall, like a string was pulling me up straight, and it helped me feel confident. After Kelly's interview, I got on my mark behind a curtain and my montage began. I heard my voice talking about how I felt when I was three hundred pounds. I glanced at the photos of me on a monitor and I got sad, but I knew I couldn't take sadness out on stage with me. I had to be positive. I looked away. The guys behind stage kept looking at the monitor and then at me, their faces skewed in disbelief. Yes, I wanted to tell them. That was me. This is me. We're the same person inside, just not on the outside.

Then I heard Oprah say something like, "Come on out!" And I did.

The audience clapped, some (probably Shari) cheered. I smiled and waved a little (at least I think I did) and hugged Bob Greene. And then there was Oprah. Oprah! She shook my hand and gave me a hug, and when I looked in her eyes, I was calm. She has the most soulful, calming eyes. I knew that anything I said up on stage, she would hear. I knew she was in the moment, not thinking about what she was going to do after the show. I was able to answer her questions as though I was talking to her at my dining room table. Before I knew it, the segment ended and the director led me to my seat in the audience.

I let out a big breath and looked around for Shari. She was sitting near the back and she waved. A few audience members smiled and gave me a thumbs up. I didn't remember much about the previous five minutes, but gauging by the response, I don't think I embarrassed myself.

After taping, everyone was relaxed and happy and full of joy and energy. So were the producers. Adrenaline was everywhere. Eventually, we collected our things and headed outside to the cars waiting to take us to the airport.

Shari's flight was in the morning, so the driver took her to a hotel which left me alone at O'Hare. I repacked my bags and changed my clothes in the bathroom before going to a kiosk to get my boarding pass. A nice woman from Ukraine helped me, but when I handed her my driver's license, she looked concerned. 'Oh no!' I thought. 'This makeover makes me look nothing like my ID!' Especially since the photo was me at three hundred pounds. I explained to her that I'd just been on *Oprah*. She said she loved *Oprah* and all was well.

Going through security, I was prepared to be questioned again, and I was, but the TSA agent thought my story was just outrageous enough to be true and he let me through.

Life quickly returned to normal, but I'm not the same person who boarded that plane to Chicago four days ago. I slayed a few dragons this week, or at least took a stab at them. I met many wonderful people, and memories keep popping up in my mind when I'm driving or cooking or working out. Was I really there? Did that really happen? Yes, it did, and I smile and shake my head and think about how strange life is sometimes.

December 2

Watching the show was a relief. In the three weeks since the taping, the details had faded, and all I remembered about being on stage was that I hugged Bob Greene and Oprah and said something about my workout.

I watched the show (with Shari, of course), and my first response was: Where the hell did those legs come from and where did I get all those teeth? I moved across the stage so deftly that I wondered if it was really me. Clearly the nervous me remained in my head and the confident me did the talking, but I'll never be ready for prime time. I wouldn't trade the experience for anything, but I'm more comfortable being the rain than the flower.

Lynn Haraldson

People, Today, & Entertainment Tonight
Posted January 2, 2008

Thank goodness Shari had a cold sore last week because I woke up with one and she told me what she used to make it go away quickly. For twenty dollars, the stuff better work.

A producer from *Today* called this morning and asked me if I'd be on the show in two days to promote *People* magazine's yearly "Half Their Size" issue that features my Lynn's Weigh blog. Unlike being on *Oprah*, this time I have to choose my own clothes, of which I have none. Well, not "none" none. I can cobble something together, I'm sure. But I have no idea about fashion, and I'm certainly no expert on what to wear on TV, so on my drug store run, I looked in the only two clothing stores in town and found a short, lined skirt that might work, but I confess I bought it mostly because of the size. I've never worn a size four.

What I'm looking forward to the most is being picked up at the airport and someone else driving me to my hotel. I drove in Manhattan years ago and believe me, no one wants me to do that again.

January 4, 2008

Morning

I forgot how loud New York is. It doesn't want anyone in bed before 11:30 p.m. and wants everyone awake at 5 a.m. And so I am, yawning, but in a good place.

Every morning when I open my email, there's an inspirational message from Daily Word. It helps me focus. This morning's message was particularly appropriate for today. It says, in part: "Spirit within discloses all I need to know in making what I may consider the most ordinary and extraordinary decisions. There is nothing, absolutely nothing, hidden from me or denied to me in the way of understanding…I am eager to make new discoveries, to move beyond my usual comfort zone in exploring my world."

I don't like surprises. I like to know what's ahead of me, what's expected, where I need to be, and when. However, I have no idea what's happening in two hours other than a producer named Lindsay is picking me up at my hotel and we'll walk over to Rockefeller Plaza. I keep expecting my stomach to leap into my throat in anxious anticipation of the unknown, but so far, things are calm in that region.

On the plane, I wondered what questions I might get asked on *Today* and also on *Entertainment Tonight* (they sprung that one on me yesterday). I thought about specific aspects of my weight-loss journey—how I felt and when, what I did to lose weight and when—and then I realized that *I'm the expert on me*. There are no questions anyone can ask that pertains to me that I can't answer. What a relief! Of course, this means I have more time to worry about lipstick stuck to my teeth or falling off my boots. God forbid I be completely anxiety-free.

I bought the *People* magazine at the Pittsburgh Airport and paged through it, looking for me, unsure of what I'd find. They'd hired a photographer who came to my house to take photos and I didn't get to see them before he left. When I got to the page, there was nothing complicated about it, just a photo of me sitting on my couch looking like myself, and the "before" photo of me taken on top of Whiteface Mountain in the Adirondacks. I was relieved. On the second page are photos and excerpts from my blog. Again, no surprises.

It's now almost 6 a.m. There will be no room service this morning, although French toast sounds really good. The hot water is brewed and the green tea I brought from home is steeping. I also brought a banana and orange, some whole grain crackers and powdered peanut butter, and a raw sugar packet for my tea. That ought to hold me until after the interviews.

January 4

Part 1

When I got to the lobby of the hotel to wait for a producer, I saw a woman who looked familiar. It was Courtney, one of the women on the cover of *People*. It was nice to have a few minutes to talk with her before we left. She was warm and kind, and if she was nervous, she didn't show it.

In the green room, which is not green, were several guests waiting for their on-air spot. Coffee, fruit, vegetables, and pastries were laid out on a large table. Several couches faced two large TV monitors hung on either side of the room. The lights were muted and soft. Further in the green room were three dressing rooms and three chairs for hair and makeup. The lights there were very bright. Courtney and I changed into our on-air clothes and compared weight-loss battle scars and exercise regimens. When we were done and waiting for hair and makeup, I looked at the name on a hand-written tag taped to the dressing room next to us.

"Courtney," I whispered. "Look who's in the dressing room next to us."

She turned around and saw Bob Saget's name. We giggled like little kids.

I got my hair done while Courtney was in makeup. Meanwhile, Bob Saget entered the room. He was drinking coffee and talking to a producer. I didn't realize he was so tall. Nice looking, too. He took the seat next to me and he talked like any normal person. Soon my hair was done, Bob's makeup was done, and it was my turn in the makeup chair.

When we were ready, Lindsay went over the script and assured

Courtney and I that the interview would be like having a conversation with a friend. The questions were straight-forward, no surprises, but I was getting a little nervous (OK, a little more than a little nervous) and tried too hard to remember why I started to lose weight, when I started my website, why I started a website, and all those other things that are rote for me at any other time. I was able to steal a moment alone to clear my head and remember who I am—literally, who I am, as in my name and where I'm from. It was like turning off your computer when it freezes and waiting 10 seconds to turn it on again.

With my shit together, we were off to the studio and entered during a break. It's not a very big space, but it's bright and cheery. Feels like someone's living room, only with cameras everywhere and a crowd peering in the windows. Like the green room, the atmosphere was laid-back and well-organized. Things happened quickly, but I didn't feel rushed or in the way. There was also no feeling of ego.

While the sound guy hooked up my microphone (thankfully he had warm hands), Lindsay showed me how I was to enter the set during my segment, and within a few minutes, I was chatting with Natalie Morales, and it really was like having a conversation with friends. Cameras? Crowd? It was just me, my old size 30/32 pants (with an embarrassing hole in the crotch that I didn't notice before) and a few other people chatting about weight.

Part 2

After the *Today* segment, the people from *People*, a makeup artist named Andrea, and I made our way through a windy underground tunnel to the Time building and the *People* offices where I'd be doing the spot for *Entertainment Tonight*. I felt like a kid following her parents. I had no idea where I was going, and I had a hard time keeping up. (Do all New Yorkers walk that fast?) Sandwich shops and lots of people walking and talking on cell phones is about all I can remember.

At the Time building's security desk, they asked to see my ID. I showed them my new driver's license. I had my old one along, too, the one from when I weighed three hundred pounds, and I showed them. Then, my mouth turned into a sieve and I told them how I had to beg the DMV to issue me a new license because I was unable to cash a check anymore, and that I almost couldn't purchase a bottle of wine because the clerk didn't believe it was me in the photo...I was rambling. I was nervous.

At the *People* offices, Andrea said she had several faces to do that day, so she set up shop on a conference table. We talked about her family home in Jamaica and menopause and dry skin. She bought me a bag of Baked Lays from the vending machine because all I had was a five-dollar bill and no change. I'll probably never see Andrea again, but what a joy it was to have known her for a moment.

Three other production people from I-don't-know-where were in the conference room with Andrea and me waiting to set up their own shoot. One of the guys told me his grandparents were from Slovakia and had worked in the southern Pennsylvania coal mines. He and his wife had also done Weight Watchers together a few years before. They both lost some weight. He seemed happy.

I loved all the accents and the diversity. Like Chicago, there are so many people living and working in Manhattan from all over. It was a humbling reminder that I'm only a miniscule part of this vast world. It's easy to forget that living in a small town.

The *ET* folks were ready for me. In a windowless studio-like room, I sat in a director's chair. There was a producer, a cameraman, a sound man, and another man — a director, perhaps — who looked like Samuel L. Jackson and sounded like Barry White. Oh my. The producer sat in a chair by the camera and interviewed me off camera. They were all kind and I was beginning to understand why everyone was like this, both at *Today* and *ET*. If I'm nervous, I can't give a good interview.

The sound guy attached my microphone and lightly put a cord with a piece of tape on it on my chest. He asked me to press it on to my shirt.

"You don't want to do it?" I asked, meaning only that I wouldn't prevent him from doing his job.

"Well, only if you want me to," he said.

"Well, you wouldn't be the first guy with a microphone up my shirt today," I said.

I didn't (exactly) mean it the way it came out, but everyone laughed, and Samuel L. Jackson said, in his delicious Barry voice, "We may need to discuss that later!" Because that made me laugh, too, I was relaxed, and I think they got the interview they were looking for.

With that, my media campaign was over and I was free to leave the building. Free to leave New York. But I had one more important thing to do: lunch with someone I'd never met.

Tracie and I met through Weight Watchers online, and when we discovered we both loved Glen Phillips and Toad the Wet Sprocket, it sealed our cyber friendship. She was one of the most confident people I'd never met. We made plans to meet for lunch near my hotel, but after walking through the underground tunnel earlier, I was turned around and I wasn't sure how to get there, so I called her and she "walked" with me until I had it in my sights.

Meeting her was more fun than I imagined and I wasn't ready to leave, but a car would be waiting soon to take me to the airport. She walked me to the hotel and we said goodbye. Unlike all the other folks I met that day, I will see Tracie again.

Part 3

The ride to LaGuardia was much different than the ride to the hotel the night before. While efficient, the driver to the hotel said few words. The driver to the airport Friday was the complete opposite. I not only know his name, marital status, and where he grew up, I know how to get licensed and insured as a driver in New York City, how many Yellow Cabs are on the streets of Manhattan at any given time, and the best way to get to LaGuardia from E. 53rd (take the Queensboro Bridge and not the tunnel, apparently).

A native New Yorker, he talked a mile a minute. The following is a portion of the conversation. Read it with a Brooklyn accent and in almost one breath: "I've had Matt Lauer riding in my car three times now and I didn't know it until my girlfriend said to me she said, 'Hey, that was Matt Lauer in your car,' and I said, 'Who's Matt Lauer?' and she says, 'What do you mean who's Matt Lauer? He's from the *Today* *s*how.' And I'm like, 'I don't watch the *Today s*how.' Then when he was in my car again I said, 'You're Matt Lauer.' Mia Farrow was in my car, too, and I thought about asking her about Woody Allen and then I thought that might not be a good idea. She's got some adopted kids, right? She looks old. I'm movin' in with my girlfriend on the fourteenth and I got the key to prove it." He shook a keychain to show me.

I learned he divorced his ex-wife, who cheated on him, and now he's in a relationship with the before mentioned girlfriend, who apparently is on Weight Watchers because she wants to look good for their wedding, but he tells her she looks great the way she is. While he was talking, his ex-wife called and he answered the phone, "Hel-loooooo. I told you to never call me at work. Didn't I tell you that? I tell you that all the time. Don't call me at work. Call me AFTER 9! Goooooobyyyyye." Click.

I thought that conversation only happened on TV.

Another ex-girlfriend works at the airport, he said. He was also in the first Gulf War, Desert Storm, in artillery; said he, "Killed my enemy from nine miles away," caught some shrapnel, and was sent home.

All this on a half-hour ride to LaGuardia. There's more, but I can't remember it all. He did, however, keep his car well stocked with water and Dove candy.

Common Ground

I checked my bag, sat down at the bar near my gate, and logged on to the Internet. The women behind me were discussing Somalia and the manager called security on a guy who was drunk and obnoxious. The suits next to me talked about women and their latest sales conquest. My head was spinning, and not from the glass of wine. I was ready to be back in Pittsburgh.

I love flying at night. It's the only time I'm glad to have a window seat. The stars above, and the intermittent lights and sometimes wide swaths of darkness below are calming. Just as I fell asleep, we landed.

I wandered a bit, but I finally found my Jeep in extended parking. As I heaved my suitcase into the back, I smacked the side of my head on the hatch. I saw stars and had to hang on to the hatch for a moment before feeling strong enough to close it. Walking to the driver's side, I felt blood trickling down my face.

"Oh, for cryin' out loud," I said to no one. I put my gloved hand to my face just as the blood curled over my lip. Inside, I found some tissues in the glove box and wiped up. I was freezing and cursing, then I started laughing. What if I'd actually passed out? I was parked in the middle of nowhere, it was twenty degrees outside, and I was wearing a sweater. No coat, no hat, no scarf. By the time my kids or airport security or some poor sap returning from Aruba found me, I'd have been frozen to the pavement.

I was staying at my daughter Cassie's that night, and when I arrived, she, being a nurse, cleaned my wound, said I could probably stand a stitch or two, and smeared some antibacterial cream on it. I was tired and hungry so I opted to forgo stitches. Except for a slight headache, a small goose egg, and a little caked blood, I was fine.

We ate dinner, watched *ET*, and the tension of the day eased. I took my granddaughter upstairs to change her diaper.

The nightlight was soft and soothing. Claire lay on her changing table, not happy at first, but I kissed her face and tickled her belly. She kicked and smiled. I stopped moving and just stared at her. My tears fell on her little torso as I changed her diaper and put on her pajamas. I told her how much I loved her and how happy I was to be her Grammy, and how nothing else in the world mattered more.

CNN
Posted January 2008

One of the first things CNN cameraman Mark Biello did when he walked into my daughter's house on Thursday was introduce himself to Sadie the dog (who barked and ran away) and to Moose the cat. Then he asked me if there was a milk or orange juice container in the refrigerator.

Being the good hostess, I asked which he preferred and went to the cupboard for a glass.

"No," he explained. "I need the plastic ring from the lid and about three feet of dental floss. Oh, and a knife or scissor."

Curious, I handed him the orange juice, dug out some dental floss from my purse, and handed him a steak knife. He cut one side of the ring and then tied on the dental floss.

"I invented this when I was living in Germany. You want to cut the ring so their paw doesn't get caught," was all the explanation I got.

Hanging on to the other end of the dental floss, Mark flung the ring at the cat and began running around the house with Moose in hot pursuit.

CNN producer Chris Hrubesh stood in the kitchen with me, smiling, his arms crossed and casual. Chris looks a little like David Caruso. He's Czech, I found out later, and he likes cannoli. He's two years younger than me and has covered stories all over the world, mostly the West Bank, Kuwait, and Israel, where he witnessed a suicide bombing in Tel Aviv. A few days before coming to Pittsburgh, both men were on the campaign trail in New Hampshire talking to Hillary Clinton and Barack Obama. Now they were in my daughter's home in a Pittsburgh suburb interviewing me because I lost a few pounds. Not worldly stuff and hardly unique. Heck, it's hardly even interesting. But they were there nonetheless, doing their job, or at least preparing to do their job. Mark was still running around with the cat.

Nothing about that moment in the kitchen was what I expected when I agreed to be part of CNN's Fit Nation. I guess I really didn't know *what* to expect, but a cameraman being chased around the house by a large orange tabby was definitely not it. I understand now that I was unwittingly being put at ease, and it worked.

The hours that followed were filled with easy, thoughtful, and comical conversation, and I gave the easiest interview to-date because Chris and Mark coax calm. I suspect they don't hear "no" very often.

Mark and Chris are smooth, not in a devious way, but intellectually smooth. They are experientially rich, but their experiences still fascinate them in almost a naïve way. I've met some interesting people in the last few months, but these two guys from CNN are by far the most fascinating.

After scoping out the best place to set up (and commenting on the Gumby cookie jar in the kitchen), Mark and Chris hauled in their equipment. Cassie was sitting on the couch, holding Claire, and we all talked about politics, native foods and alcohol of various foreign countries, the blight of the British Empire, and the time Mark was in Clarion in the mid-1980s for a friend's wedding, a large Slovakian event with lots of vodka and potatoes and cabbage.

We also discussed our love of Chris Farley. Chris said his favorite Farley SNL character was Matt Foley, motivational speaker ("I live in a van down by the river!"). This led us to sing a few lines from Lunch

Lady Land, too ("Sloppy joes, sloppy, sloppy joes…hoagies and grinders, hoagies and grinders…navy beans navy beans…").

While setting up a tall light next to my chair, Mark said, "Sixteen years ago today I was filming the bombs dropping on Baghdad."

I thought for a second. "Wait," I said. "Wasn't that seventeen years ago?"

"Huh," laughed Mark. "It's 2008, isn't it?"

Mark (aka Mad Dog) was one of a small group of CNN reporters who were in Baghdad covering Desert Storm in 1991. I remember that night vividly, watching CNN, scared, wondering when it would end. How astonishing to think that the man shooting the video that night in Baghdad was now turning his camera on little old me. Whether it's fate or coincidence or quantum physics, the world was very small and very simple at that moment.

Mark and his colleagues' experience was turned into an HBO film *Live From Baghdad* starring Michael Keaton, Helena Bonham Carter, and Joshua Leonard, who played Mark. Mark was an advisor on the set during filming.

"It was fun," he said matter-of-factly. Then he told me about the time he had dinner with Saddam Hussein at his palace, and how complicated eating was for the dictator because people were always trying to poison him. I wondered if Saddam had a cat and if Mark made it a plastic ring-dental floss toy. That's when I realized that I was two degrees of separation from Saddam Hussein! And I thought meeting Oprah was mind-blowing.

Mark and Chris were in Louisiana during Hurricane Katrina. Chris reported from Slidell and Mark was in New Orleans where, as he was working, saved more than a dozen lives. He said it as though he does that kind of thing every day.

Just before our interview, Chris said the guy he interviewed the day before had lost more than one hundred ninety pounds and that he'd cried during the interview. I told Chris that nothing he said would make me cry. Then he found the photo of Cassie and me from the day she graduated from basic training in 2002. It was in a frame on the bookshelf. I told him how hard that summer was, saying goodbye to Cassie, waiting weeks before she could call, and when she did, how we spent the entire five minutes crying, barely saying a word. I teared up. Chris smiled.

"I knew I could get you to cry," he said.

During the actual interview, the phone rang once and Claire squawked for a second, but otherwise it was quiet. I looked at Chris the whole time, fighting my natural impulse to look away when someone looks me in the eyes for longer than a few seconds.

When we were done with the interview, they filmed me walking up and down the stairs and walking the dog in the snow. Mark gained Sadie's trust, and he threw her Giggly-Wiggly ball over and over again. Chris and I stood by their van until they were done.

As they packed up to leave, I noticed they used a particularly large case that they stuffed with most of the things that had been in the living room a few minutes before.

"It's called the Widow Maker," said Chris. I could see why. It weighs eighty pounds, and while it's on wheels, it still needs to be lifted in and out of vehicles and up and down stairs. I said it's probably a hernia maker, too. Chris said that was a concern for many of the guys who haul the Widow Maker around.

Mark gave Cassie and me CNN caps and Claire got a little News Hound stuffed dog. They said they were going to Station Square that evening. Cassie recommended Bar Louis.

"Martinis, eh?" said Mark with a grin. Chris rolled his eyes and said he wanted to work out in the hotel gym first. We hugged goodbye and they said if we were ever in Atlanta that they'd give us a tour.

Lynn Haraldson

No More Apologies
Posted October 2010

"I notice you apologize a lot," a friend told me the other day.

"I do?" I said. "I'm sorry."

"See?" he laughed. "You did it again!"

It's true, I apologize a lot. It comes mostly from a skewed sense of space I take up in the world or a room or next to someone. I've always been painfully aware of my physical presence, at any weight, and have struggled most of my life with feeling physically flawed. Long ago, these feelings manifested into spatial form, and even after years of therapy and despite this weight loss, I sometimes feel unworthy to occupy the space I need.

In high school, I weighed about one hundred fifty pounds and I did everything I could to hide what I thought was a large body. I stayed as small and unnoticeable as I could by walking slightly slumped over and with my arms wrapped tightly around my books, I rarely wore heels, and I crossed my legs wherever I sat.

I also was easy to sleep with (not in the Biblical sense). When I was young, I unconsciously trained myself to take up as little space as I could in a bed. To this day, I don't move around much, and I usually wake up in the same position as I fell asleep—on my side in a somewhat fetal position, hugging a pillow. Even now, particularly in the presence of someone with a strong personality and/or outer beauty, I try to be as invisible as possible.

A recent example was when I went to see a friend's new band perform. As he tuned his guitars and plugged in the amps, the singer, Molly, walked up to the bar where I was sitting and ordered a beer. I introduced myself and we chatted for about fifteen minutes.

A lovely young woman in her late twenties, Molly radiates kindness. She's also lithe thin and graceful with long arms, long legs, long fingers, and a swanlike neck. As we talked at the bar, I caught myself hunching my shoulders and squeezing my crossed legs tighter together. When I checked in with my body (something mindfulness meditation has taught me to do), I realized I felt really large sitting next to her, and my posture was my way of apologizing.

When Molly left to warm up, I checked in with my mind and it was thinking that I, too, have long legs, long arms, and long fingers, but they are attached to unacceptably broad shoulders and broad hips. My neck is thick and susceptible to sagging. Negative upon negative. Apology on top of apology.

Rather than be disheartened, I got curious. Curious *and*, more importantly, non-judgmental. *Tonight, I will not be invisible*. I released my legs from their cramped position and let the blood flow back to my feet. I sat up straight and lowered my shoulders.

It's a work in progress, staying visible. I intuitively sleep without moving, and still catch myself shrinking into myself when I feel intimidated or weak. I say the words, "I'm sorry" without thinking about why I'm sorry. But checking in with my body and mind, and sensing all there is to sense, feeling its source when it's fresh rather than when it's days, months, or years old, is a huge breakthrough.

There are many times I wanted to be invisible in the last three years, but it wouldn't have been prudent for me to run away. Facing this fear really started with *Oprah*. How in the world did I get through meeting her without begging the earth to swallow me up? I obviously drew from something inside — something I was not aware of at the time, but I credit my friend Shari for tapping into it. During our trip to Chicago, she talked me down from a lot of self-doubt and wasn't afraid to tell me to pull my head out of my butt and see the big picture, and to maybe, just maybe, have some fun.

This personal strength is something I need and want to cultivate to live in the light rather than in the shadows. I don't want to be invisible and I don't want to physically shrink in the presence of beauty or strength.

While I doubt I can change my sleeping habits, I want to fill up my necessary space and stop apologizing for who I am. I want to feel the aliveness of awareness and take in what strength and beauty has to offer.

So here's to sitting straight, uncrossing my legs, unfolding my arms, and embracing something larger and more significant than a pillow.

Unless, of course, you don't agree.

Just kidding!

6. Biking

"The bicycle will inspire women with more courage, self-respect, and self-reliance and make the next generation more vigorous of mind and body."

— Elizabeth Cady Stanton

"When the spirits are low, when the day appears dark, when work becomes monotonous, when hope hardly seems worth having, just mount a bicycle and go out for a spin down the road, without thought on anything but the ride you are taking."

— Sir Arthur Conan Doyle

The same week I began working on this chapter, the limericks portion of NPR's *Wait Wait…Don't Tell Me!* featured one that summed it up perfectly:

My helmet, I don't really like.
But for spandex and foot clips, I'm psyched.
And my soul is aflame for that ultra-light frame.

Lynn Haraldson

I am deeply in love with my bike.

While I don't usually wear spandex or use foot clips, and I prefer a hybrid over a road bike, the sentiment is the same. What started out as a fun outdoor exercise after losing a substantial amount of weight turned into an emotional connection that I liken to a friendship and, at times, therapy. Biking took me to "thin spaces" where the secular meets the sacred, places I would never have seen on foot or in my car.

As these essays will testify, I really am in love with my bike(s).

Bike Envy
Posted May 2007

Twenty years ago, a group of boys in a car mooed as they drove by me riding a bike. Instead of defending myself to myself or at least giving myself a shred of credit for even being on a bike that day, I gave them what little self-esteem I had and didn't ride a bike again.

In the years since, I've envied people like my husband who ride their bikes with such ease, hardly seeming to break a sweat, even on hills, just like I did when I was a kid.

Older, wiser, and with more courage than I had twenty years ago, I decided last week that I was ready to get back on a bike. On Saturday, my husband and I went to a bike shop and I took a few out for a test drive, proving to myself that riding a bike is like riding a bike. You never forget.

The bike I selected is technically a "boy's" bike. It fit me better than a bike without a bar. To even things out, I bought a pink backpack and a pink water bottle.

We chose as our first official ride together a stretch of road in Cook Forest State Park that winds along the Clarion River. For seven of the nine years we've been married, I was not physically active at all, so I was afraid I wouldn't be able to keep up. I should have had more faith in myself (and in my husband). I had no problems aerobically or with endurance, and except for having to wear a helmet, I felt like a kid again!

We started at the Cooksburg Post Office and turned around five miles later at the Clarion River Lodge, where my daughter was married last August. I've driven on that road hundreds of times, but being on a bike slowed down time, and I could better appreciate the ducks and the swallows, the hills and rocks, and the small white rapids on the river. The dense, fresh smell of the forest floor and the hemlocks was less fleeting. When we got back to the car, I felt renewed, forgiven (for what I don't know, but that's how it felt), and empowered.

I wish I hadn't let those boys get to me the way they did, but the years weren't for naught. Their cruelty helped fuel my need to reassemble my self-esteem, and I've practiced in my head what I'd say (or gesture) if they come around again.

I Know I Can
Posted May 2011

Yesterday, I went for my first official bike ride of the season and the first one since my divorce. Still friends, my ex-husband joined me, and I played host by choosing the trail and driving.

In the four years we biked together, loading the bikes on the rack was always Larry's job. When I went on a solo ride, there was room for my bike in the back of my old Jeep, although one or more body parts always got cut or bruised during the loading and unloading. My newer Jeep is smaller, and with two car seats practically welded into the back seat, there's no room for a bike. I had to learn to manage a rack, so last month I bought a used one that fits over the spare tire. I practiced several times in the driveway loading and unloading my bike and felt pretty confident I could load two. When Larry arrived, I told him I didn't want to need help, and he stood back as I put the bike rack securely on the tire, loaded our bikes, and secured them with bungee cord and a strap. To his credit, Larry didn't check my work, as I thought he might. I drove to the trailhead without incident.

We covered eleven miles in an hour and change. This was down from our usual average of thirteen to fifteen miles in an hour, but my body is different this year and so is my focus. I chose to start at a trailhead six miles west of the start of the trail, which put us in the downhill slope first. I prefer to do the uphill work first, but because this this was my first ride of the season and my body was crankier than usual, I had zero confidence that I could bike more than a few minutes or a few miles, especially on an unfamiliar surface—crushed limestone—so taking it easy the first half of the ride seemed prudent.

As bad as his eyesight is, Larry is an excellent birder. He can always spot the smallest of birds, even when he's in motion. Yesterday on the trail, he stopped suddenly when he saw a scarlet tanager and I nearly ran into him. I didn't see it before it flew away. So disappointing, but a half mile later, Larry stopped again. "Look! An indigo bunting! See it? See it?" This time, I saw it. And it was beautiful and brave and didn't move even though we were just a few feet from him.

We turned around after five and a half miles. It wasn't going to be too difficult of an uphill ride, but it would be constant, and given I'm not the cardio queen I was a year ago, I was a little worried. But hey, what goes down, must go up, and I'd been down long enough. I took off the thin, long-sleeved shirt I wore over my t-shirt, tucked my Blackberry in my pocket, and started peddling.

Minutes in, the lung rush and the increased heartbeat started, but it was familiar, like an old friend. I knew what was being asked of my body. I'd been there before. And despite a lack-luster, half-assed winter of "exercise," I felt incredible. I stopped a few times to take photos, but most of the time I peddled and peddled and peddled. When I got back to the Jeep, I was a sweaty, stinky, happy-beyond-belief mess.

I've been on dozens of rides in four years, but this was the most spiritual. It renewed my faith in my physical self, and it affirmed what I've been trying to accept for many months — that less is better and that there is balance between doing everything and doing nothing.

Fast Star
Posted May 2011

After impressing my granddaughter Claire with my bike rack/bike tying skills ("Oooohhh, Grammy! My bike is so safe! It won't fall off!"), I buckled her in her car seat and we were off to the bike trail. Part of our conversation along the way: "I love my baby sister. We get to keep her!" along with her asking and me answering *at least* thirty times "Are we there yet?"

From the moment Cassie threw her positive pregnancy test stick on my menu at Applebee's, I dreamed of this day: teaching my grandchild the joys of riding a bike on a trail, and today's ride was everything I'd dreamed and more.

Claire — three and a half years old and three and a half feet tall — has taught me more about myself than any human ever has. As we rode today, with me riding alongside her and protecting her from the edge ("You're high up there, Grammy! You have a big bike."), I felt not only the responsibility of being a grandparent, but an even greater love for her than I can possibly explain.

Claire named her bike Fast Star. As she peddled along the path at around 3.8 mph, once in a while she'd yell, "Go, Fast Star! Go fast!" and get her speed up to 5.1. Talk about keeping me balanced on my peddling toes.

"Don't run over the worms, Grammy!"

"There's a cardinal!"

"What's that butterfly, Grammy?"

"A swallowtail," I said.

"A shwallatale."

"Yup."

We turned around after one mile and got halfway back when Claire asked, "Where's the parking lot, Grammy? My legs are getting tired." We stopped for a break and chatted about worms and butterflies and what kind of ice cream she was going to get at Del's. When we got back on our bikes, Fast Star wasn't quite as fast as when we started, and Claire wasn't as chatty.

"Are we there yet?"

"Soon."

We stopped to look at the creek, and Claire seemed to get her second wind. "Can we play down there?"

Next time, I promised.

"OK!" and she and Fast Star "raced" me back to the parking lot.

Common Ground

Zen and the Art of Bicycle Maintenance
Posted June 2011

> *"Like those in the valley behind us, most people stand in sight of the spiritual mountains all their lives and never enter them, being content to listen to others who have been there and thus avoid the hardships."*
>
> —From *Zen and the Art of Motorcycle Maintenance*

Biking is a "spiritual mountain" to me, and I'm not content to merely stand in the sight of that mountain. But I needed a lesson in listening to others who've been to that mountain to learn how I might avoid some of the hardships.

Last week, on the last leg of the Butler-Freeport Trail, I'd traveled six miles farther than I planned. I was hungry, but I hadn't packed any snacks. Nine miles from my car, I ran over a rock that I thought punctured my tire. Thankfully it didn't, but it occurred to me that it would be a really good idea to learn something about bike maintenance.

Enter Lori and Kyle. Lori, a fellow blogger, is an avid biker so I asked her what she takes along when she rides, and how I might go about seeking advice on bicycle maintenance.

"First off," she wrote, "if you are by yourself, the one thing you should do is tell someone where you are going — or at least close to the general vicinity.

"I have a bike bag on the back of my bike. I always take: cell phone, spare tube, small hand pump (or CO_2 cartridge inflators), tire lifters (small plastic wedges to remove tires), something like hard candy in case I am out too long, and water. For long rides, I also include a bike lock, food, sunscreen, anti-chafing cream, hand sanitizer, and chain lube.

"I would also practice taking off your tire at home so that if it happens in the field, it won't be the first time. Most bike shops will have free classes on tire changing and maintenance, so definitely check them out!

"I would also recommend a book called *Every Woman's Guide to Cycling*. See if your library can get it for you."

I Googled bike shops in my area and found Michael's Cycles: "Independent shop on the outskirts of town…We are a small, family-run business that treats everyone to courteous service. One of the biggest complaints we hear about bike shops is that if you aren't wearing spandex, you get ignored. Well, not here." I knew this was the place.

I chose to go to Michael's Cycles a few days later after a sweaty two-mile hike through horse- and deer-fly infested woods in 88-degree heat. A good sweat makes me more confident, and I knew that I needed all the confidence I could muster because whenever I set out to do this kind of thing alone, my insecurity comes along for the ride, keeping me just off balance enough that I feel a nagging sense of self-doubt.

It was just my luck that when I pulled into the parking lot, a young man was putting a bike rack on the top of a male customer's car. I like men, but their Y chromosome makes me nervous sometimes. It's a reaction born from years of teasing, put downs, and ignorance from the opposite sex that I fight all the time: I'll be judged/stared at/laughed at/criticized.

The customer was sweaty, like he'd just been on a ride. He was about my age and nice looking, which intimidates me even more. But I bucked up and walked across the lot. "I am responsible for how I allow myself to be treated," I told myself. "You are a woman who bikes, not a woman with baggage."

As I approached them, the young man looked down from the bike rack and smiled. "Hi! What can I help you with?"

"I used to bike with someone, but I don't anymore. I need to know some things about bike maintenance. Do you guys do that kind of thing?"

"Oh heck, yeah!" he said. "I'm Kyle. If you've got some time right now, I'll show you how to change your tire when I'm done here."

"I have an appointment this afternoon, but are you around tomorrow?" I asked.

"Yeah, after twelve," he said, jumping off the top of the customer's car. "I'll get you a card."

As he walked into the shop, I turned to the customer and apologized for taking Kyle away from his bike rack installation. The man smiled and said it was no problem and asked if I'd heard of the Butler-Freeport Trail. *Yay!* I thought. *Common ground!* The insecurities I had disappeared as he talked to me as a person who bikes. I felt on equal ground.

The next day, I took my bike to the shop and Kyle showed me how to change a tube, and offered tips on maintenance. I am now the proud owner of a 700-by-35/40 inner tube, three tire levers, a portable air pump (which Kyle mounted on my bike), and a primo pressure gauge that works with both Schrader and Presta valves (and I know what each of them is).

From *Zen...*: "In a car you're always in a compartment, and because you're used to it you don't realize that through that car window everything you see is just more TV. You're a passive observer and it is all moving by you boringly in a frame. On a cycle the frame is gone. You're completely in contact with it all. You're in the scene, not just watching it anymore, and the sense of presence is overwhelming."

I've spent too much time avoiding that which scares me, and by moving forward in spite of my fears and not waiting for them to dissolve, I've discovered the beauty of self-empowerment. Not only do I learn something, like a concrete skill or something about myself, I change something about myself. Not a bad way to spend this time in my life.

The Best Worst Bike Ride Ever
Posted June 2011

I checked the radar, and all I saw was a little green blip forty miles southwest of my house. I got dressed, did some strength training, then headed outside and loaded up the bike.

I was going to ride my favorite little fourteen-miler. The first half is a nice gradual incline, one I like to do at about nine to eleven mph, then I turn around and ride somewhat downhill at about thirteen mph.

The temperature was a perfect seventy-four degrees and there was a nice breeze. I pulled into the parking lot and saw Creepy House Owner who lives next to the parking lot of the trailhead. He was talking to a fellow biker who was loading his bike. I got out of my car and hoped Fellow Biker would keep Creepy House Owner busy until I unloaded and started riding.

Such was not my luck. Creepy House Owner, with his five-day beard and tobacco breath, came up to me and said, *while reaching out to touch me*, "Those look like rain clouds coming in."

I shrugged him off my shoulder and worked as fast as I could to undo the straps and lift my bike off the rack.

"Yeah, well, I won't shrink," I said. I locked my car and hopped on my bike before he could touch me again. I didn't get out my iPod until he was well out of sight.

Two miles in, I was in my stride and enjoying the breeze and the dense foliage that has filled in so beautifully along the trail. Three miles in, I felt a few drops of rain. No biggie. I kept going. The rain got a little steadier a half mile later, and I stopped under a tree to wait it out.

I didn't take out my phone to check the radar (as that would have been the prudent thing to do) because, as those of you who've know me longer than five minutes know, I'm as patient as a two-year-old sometimes. Three minutes under the tree, the rain was still sputtering and I decided I'd waited long enough, I'll ride it out.

I hopped on my bike and continued up the trail. Another mile in, the sputtering turned steady and I was getting pretty wet. Frustrated, I turned around and headed back. Nine miles would be all today.

A half mile later, the steady rain turned into a sheet of rain and my bike was kicking up so much dirt into my mouth and eyes I had a hard time seeing the trail.

I knew there was a shelter a few miles from the parking lot, so I peddled as fast as I could, never getting below fifteen mph.

That is, until I saw the fawn.

She was a lovely little thing, standing on the trail looking toward me. I slowed down to admire her.

The rain poured over me, but I was already soaked and it was never that I'd ever seen a deer on the...

Crack! Boom!

Yikes! Lightning struck really close and I was really not close to the shelter. I had at least a mile to go. I cranked on my bike like I was being chased by the devil. I was flying as it poured, and I was having the time of my life. Soaking wet and cold, but damn, I proved I could be fast when I needed to be.

I saw the shelter up ahead and part of a bike sticking out. I remembered passing one other biker on the trail. A man. I debated: Do I stop or keep going? Stop or keep...

CRACK!

I stopped.

"Holy crap!" I laughed as I got off my bike. "It's really raining out here!"

I looked down at myself and saw to my total embarrassment that, well, I was in a t-shirt and I was cold. You know, *cold* cold. I crossed my arms nonchalantly over my chest as the man moved over so I could sit down. If he saw how "cold" I was, he never let on.

He had a kind face; a short graying beard and soft eyes. He looked younger than me, but I found out later he just turned fifty. He opened his pack and handed me a couple of paper towels (I only carry tissues). I thanked him and began drying off my arms and face. We exchanged first names and what-do-you-do's and rode out the rain with pleasant conversation.

He's been riding for a few years, and had converted a 1970s ten-speed Schwinn road bike into a six-speed mountain-type bike. It was really cool looking. He asked if I'd ever ridden the Great Allegheny Passage Trail. No, I said, but it's on my riding bucket list. He told me about his favorite section of the trail and how it wound through several small towns.

"You'll think you're in Mayberry!" he said.

Mr. Shelter Guy was funny, smart, and articulate, and when the sun came out, we talked a little longer. Not a bad way to ride out a storm. He asked for my blog site, but since neither of us had paper or a pen, I told him to Google my name.

We got back on our bikes and he went his way and I went mine. I called over my shoulder, "Hey, if you find me online, write if you'd like a biking partner!" I think he yelled back, "OK!" but maybe that's because it's what I wanted to hear. I don't mind biking alone, but it would be fun to go with someone once in a while.

When I got back to the parking lot, I was even muddier than I was at the shelter, and Creepy House Owner was there waiting. I'll tell you what, I've never put my bike on the rack so fast as I did today, and I did it while not allowing him to invade my personal space again. I mean, really. Who touches a stranger like that?

When I got home, I put my bike in the garage and closed the garage door. I stripped as soon as I was inside, and got in the shower to hose off.

I'm not sure I got all the dirt out of my hair, and I'm pretty sure I'll be digging black specks out of my eyes for the next several hours, but I'm pumped. Today's ride was, by far, the best worst ride of my biking career. Even though that green blip grew into a massive red blob on the radar, hitting the trail was a really good idea.

Clearing My Head
Posted March 2012

This morning, I took one hell of an online test in Medical Nutrition Therapy as part of a program in dietetics I applied to a few months ago. Math was involved. And it was timed. Afterwards, I was shaking and second guessing myself and saying things like, "Ugh! I'm stupid. I'll never pass."

It was sixty-something degrees outside. Sunny, but a bit windy, with twenty-five mph gusts. I'd been up studying since 6 a.m. I watched the sun rise. I checked the weather a million times on my phone and I thought about Bike. I've been eyeing her every time I pull in my garage, wondering if she misses me as much as I miss her. Bike needs a tune up, no doubt, but I wondered if she'd have enough oomph from last year to get me through a late winter ride.

My mind was making me nuts. I had to get out of the house, and the only place to go that made sense was the Butler-Freeport Community Trail: twenty one miles of personal peace. I worked out a whole lot of joint pain and angst there last year, and it was where I said yes to my thighs when they said, "Are you sure?" while pedaling up a two-mile incline along the outer edge of a gun range.

I had to go. I slathered Vaseline on my face to protect it from the wind and put on two shirts, a jacket, leggings, and tennis shoes. I backed the car out of the garage and loaded my bike on the rack. I felt strong and in control, even though it had been five months since my last ride.

My body felt good hugged in form-fitting clothes. The snugness reminded me that I had one. A body, that is. It wasn't lost in the perpetual layers of winter. And while I've gained twenty pounds since my lowest weight, my body feels stronger than it did at one hundred twenty five pounds. I'm no longer afraid I'll break. I felt so fragile back then.

With the sunroof open and the music cranked, I wondered if I'd be the only one on the trail, but obviously, other people were feeling like me. Several cars with bike racks were lined up in the parking lot and fortunately, Creepy House Owner was not outside.

I took my bike off the rack and examined it. I'd pumped up the tires before I left, and I had a tube and tire levers in my pack, but it had been a year since I learned how to use them. What if I got a flat? Standing there with a hand on the saddle and a hand on the handle bar, the sun warmed my back and the air smelled like spring. I decided I'd walk back if I had to. Nothing was going to stop me from riding. I got on my favorite way: with my left foot on the pedal and swinging my right leg over the seat like it was the back of a horse.

Hello, picnic table! Hello, campsite across the creek! Hello, shelter that kept me and another biker I'd never met before and haven't seen since dry in a torrential thunderstorm last year!

Hello, ice and mud and the bug that just flew into my eye! Hello, rapids! Hello, really tall bridge that looks like the Empire's Imperial Walkers and scares me every time I ride under it!

Hello, wooden mile markers! Hello, Monroe Road that I pedal like hell across because people drive around the bend like they're racing in the Daytona 500! Hello, couple walking their dog off leash! Not cool, by the way!

Hello, wind and sun and sixty five degrees! Hello, faint smell of woodsy western Pennsylvania! You'll be in full smell soon.

I rode for twenty minutes and turned around. While I wanted to go farther, I knew my body and Bike needed time to "tune up" and prepare for longer rides. I drove home in the closest thing to a perfect state of mind I could achieve.

Seven Times Slower
Posted October 2012

It's been almost a month since my last bike ride. Tethered to my calendar filled with various appointments, I've spent a lot of time logging miles in the Jeep, always with the intention of getting "there" as quickly as possible. I have been what Jon Kabat-Zinn calls a "human doing."

When I got on my bike yesterday for the first time in four weeks, ten, eleven, and twelve mph seemed really s-l-o-w. It took my brain a few miles to realize that there's a lot more to see and experience when you're biking seven times slower than driving a car.

At seven times slower, I thought about how much I love this time of year, and that despite its bittersweet theme of death and decay, I cling to its promise of rebirth. At seven times slower, I could smell and hear the leaves above, shaking on the trees, and beneath me, crunching beneath my tires

At seven times slower, I noticed a cat slinking up a hill and on the farm along the trail, a pig slept in the mud of his large pen. At seven times slower, I saw that the farmer felt it necessary to post a sign, "Do not throw objects at turkeys." What kind of person throws things at turkeys?

Anyway, at seven times slower, I said goodbye to the cows, and the power lines, and the golf course. I could feel my body release its seventy-mile-per-hour tension, fiber by fiber (even though I was still pretty irritated by the whole throwing things at turkeys).

At seven times slower, I thought to visit my daughter and grandchildren. I see them several times a week, but usually because of some need for one of them to be somewhere else. Yesterday, I sat in their presence and absorbed their essence, and I snuggled with Claire in her genuine fire fighter hat that she sleeps with like a stuffed animal.

Like the hundreds of bike rides before, this one was a gift. I was set free, if only for a few hours, and at seven times slower, I was a human "being."

It's Like Riding a Bike
Posted July 2015

Who cries when they buy a bike?

Me.

I bought a used southwestern goldish color, five-year-old Schwinn Voyageur 2 at a local bike shop on Monday. I cried when I got her home, too, but only because after I hoisted her off the bike rack I bought (that cost more than she did), the handlebar smacked me in the cheek. Happy tears/pain tears, either way, I now have a bike friend again.

My previous bike friend was a men's Giant hybrid I called Bike. We were together for seven years. I knew all her idiosyncrasies. Bike gave me confidence. She gave me strength. She helped me think. Bike made me feel less lonely and isolated after my divorce. We went on adventures to places I'd never gone alone before. She encouraged me to take chances.

The last time I rode Bike was in March 2013. I rode three miles on my favorite trail when my right knee gave out. It just stopped working. I've had surgeries and I've had babies, but never have I felt the kind of pain I felt in my knee that morning. I was on crutches for a week. When I felt better, though, I was afraid to ride again. Bike stayed perched in the garage, ready for another adventure, but I ignored her.

I moved in January 2014 and stored Bike in my boyfriend's barn. The tactile sensation of moving her and going through the contents of her saddle bag made me optimistic about riding again. One month later, Bike burned in a fire that destroyed the barn. Gone, too, was my bike rack, helmet, lock, odometer, trail maps, tubes, tire levers, air pump, and the five dollars and package of tissues I kept in the bag.

The now dull gray charred gear shaft is all that's left of Bike.

In spring 2014, I developed hip pain and I told myself that was why I couldn't go biking. Truth was, I was mourning Bike and I didn't have it in me to buy a new one.

In December, I had my hip replaced, which took away the reason I "couldn't" ride. When I saw other people biking, I got that twinge in my heart, that yearning to be them. Still, I wallowed in feeling cheated. My hip, my bike...poor me. It got to the point of ridiculous. Finally, a month ago, I went for a short walk on a beloved bike trail. I thought about Bike and wondered, *What if?* Given my propensity for adopting shelter pets, I went to a bike shop and test rode that somewhat beat-up Schwinn. The minute I started pedaling, I felt free. I felt joy. I had a physical purpose again and a partner who would challenge me to take down that "I can't" wall I'd built.

That evening, I practiced taking my bike on and off the new rack on the back of my Jeep. I researched local trails and decided on one not far away. The next morning, I drove to the Black Lick trailhead on the Hoodlebug Trail, which feeds into the Ghost Town Trail, nervously watching my bike bob up and down on every bump in the road.

I felt like I was on a blind date. I tried to be cool by unloading my bike like I'd done it a thousand times. I attached my water bottle, loaded my bag, calculated my computer/odometer thingy, locked up the Jeep, and got on my bike. I found the trailhead and rode slowly up a moderate incline.

At the top, there was a steep grade sign, only with a bike and not a truck. I love going downhill, sure, but I'd have to come back up eventually.

I negotiated briefly with my ego. I acknowledged that: A) it's been over two years since I've ridden a bike, and B) I've gained a new hip and a few pounds and I have not been exercising like I used to. Thankfully, humility was my best friend at that moment, and I gave my judging self the permission to walk my bike back up the steep incline rather than ride up.

It was eighty-four degrees and the humidity was at least one thousand percent, and the unfamiliar trail provided little shade. It was also more uphill than I anticipated. I rode for a few miles and decided to turn around. I was sad at first; betrayed and embarrassed. I stopped under a tree near a creek and had a talk with myself: "Lynn, here's the deal. You have to push yourself slowly because you're not in the same physical condition you were in two years ago. No, you won't break any land speed or distance records, and you won't be saying 'Passing left' anytime soon. You're starting from the bottom. You have no place to go but up."

I thought about the reasons I love and need to ride a bike. Not biking the past few years, I've become more of a small self, an isolated self, an egoic transient wandering from fear to fear. I crave the movement of biking, but moreover, I crave the butterflies, the dragonflies, and the indigo buntings, and swerving to avoid the chipmunks who skittishly venture out on the side of the trail. I crave the smell of the woods, the feel of the humidity clinging to my arms, the breeze that cools my skin. I need these things, and now, I am again part of them.

Today, I chose a different trail. On the West Penn Trail, I experienced that exhilarating fear of wild, of no one around, of a bear could come out of nowhere and I was completely alone. I rode without my earbuds, listening to the air and staying hyper aware of my surroundings. I heard every bird and every crush of the limestone beneath my tires. Three miles in, I turned around, even though I ached to go another two miles. I knew my legs would question that choice on the way back and I wanted to do what was best for all of me. I put in my earbuds and "turned on some music to start my day…" "More Than A Feeling" is a great riding song.

When I got back to my Jeep, I was totally high, happy, and sweaty. In the parking lot, a man was securing his bike to his car's rack and he offered to help me load mine. I thanked him and said no, that I had to get used to doing this again. We talked about the trail for a few minutes and I was reminded of another reason I love biking. People on the trails are usually really nice. I've missed that camaraderie of like-minded people. We are like ships in the night. "Good morning!" we say as we pass each other in opposite directions, "Passing left!" when we pass in the same.

I'm still part of the fellowship of people who love biking on trails, even though my thighs, arms, and neck are asking me why. I rub the aches and tell my body, "You'll get used to it." I will press on because I am not the same person I was three days ago. I am my old biking self. I am the person I've missed for two years. This used, gold-colored bike isn't Bike, but I think Bike would approve of her replacement.

7. Weight Part 2 — The B Sides

"Once I was beautiful. Now I am myself."

—Anne Sexton

From 2005 through 2010, my writing focused mostly on my experiences while losing more than one hundred seventy pounds and maintaining it. In the ensuing years, my life has changed, my body has changed, and I considered not including the B sides of my "success" story. But that felt insincere. The changes in my weight are as much a part of my story as the weight loss and is far more representative of the challenges regarding weight than my somewhat fairy-tale story of weight loss and weight maintenance.

While I am grateful for the time in the weight-loss spotlight, I was humbled by the number of people, mostly women, who described an often overwhelming desperation about their bodies. Nearly every ounce of their self-esteem revolved around a number on the scale, and it made me reconsider my relationship with weight. I began to see it less as something that had to go away and instead, as a part of the overall, complicated picture of a complete self. In time, I adopted a message of self-acceptance over militancy. I used to say, "I don't celebrate with food." Now, food isn't the enemy.

At the end of my last weight-loss journey, the real one began; the one in which I consider all of me and not just the part of me that can be measured by a number.

In the spirit of Anne Sexton, once I was many different weights. Now I am myself.

I Still Believe
Posted January 2012

In the song "I Still Believe" by The Call, Michael Been sings: *"I still believe. Through the shame and through the grief. Through the heartache and through the tears, through the waiting and through the years."* It is my theme song for determination and perseverance, and I listen to it often.

So much of what we strive to do in our lives, and what we deep down want to achieve, is in defiance of what we've been told—either by others or by ourselves—we can't do. How many times have you lost weight, only to gain it back? How many times have you started exercising, only to quit after a few months? When have you heard (and by whom), "You can't do that! You tried before and failed! Come, have a cookie."

* Raising my hand *

We all have a voice inside telling us what it thinks we should do. Sometimes it's a know-it-all smarty pants: "So-and-so will like you more if you _____." "You'll be happy if you just _____." "Life will be perfect once you have _____." But sometimes, if we think about what we really need and want, and we choose to believe in ourselves, we can create a more positive voice: "You want this for yourself." "You're worth it." "I believe in you and in this goal!"

Which voice we listen to determines whether we retreat or advance, even if it seems scary. Recently, I agreed to do something way outside my comfort zone. While I vowed I'd never be on television again promoting weight loss, I will fly to New York in early February to tape a segment on weight maintenance for *60 Minutes Australia.*

I declined the offer when I received the initial email from the producer, telling him I wasn't the poster child he might be looking for. I'd gained some weight and was struggling with arthritis so I wasn't exercising as much as I used to or in the same way. His reply made me rethink the "truths" I'd convinced myself of recently:

"May I say it sounds like you are being a little tough on yourself! You're are still half the weight you once were, and despite your body having some issues, you are still living healthily and not stacking on too many pounds. It's not so much the 'poster child' we are after, but the real story of someone who has broadly succeeded in not reverting to their former weight, and being determined about it."

Determined. I reread that word more than a few times. Had I been demonstrating determination the last few years as I've put on weight? Yes, I believed I had. I'd learned so much about weight maintenance and was determined to make it a larger part of our culture's dialogue than weight loss. In the passion of that moment, I wrote back and said I'd do it.

As soon as I clicked "send," I had a knot in the center of my stomach and I wanted to eat. But instead of consuming copious amounts of whatever, I took a bunch of deep breaths, got dressed, and went to visit my grandkids. What I realized was that the voice inside me could say all it wanted about my fear of being on television again. My will is stronger.

I still believe in me. I still believe that through the bumps in the road, through the temptations and heartaches, through the worries and self-doubts, that I can do what I (and others) tell me I can't do.

If you get a chance, listen to "I Still Believe." It's for people like us, in places like this. Dance to it in the kitchen. I still believe. I hope you do, too.

"I did dit!"
Posted March 2012

I volunteer for a non-profit agency in Pittsburgh that, among other things, operates a food pantry and soup kitchen, and prepares and delivers meals for Meals-On-Wheels.

When I'm on a Meals-On-Wheels route, I'm always the visitor and never the driver because I get turned around in the neighborhoods we service. Yesterday, I was teamed with driver Deacon Smith, a retired postal worker who's been with MOW for twenty years. He's a kind, laid-back man who knows Route 3 like the back of his hand.

Our first stop was an apartment complex where two clients live. The instruction was that if we didn't reach one client in her apartment, she was likely at the other's. When I rang the lobby buzzer for one and didn't get an answer, I rang the buzzer for the other and was let in. When I got to the apartment, I knocked and called out, "Meals On Wheels!"

"Come on in! Door's unlocked!" replied a voice inside.

I walked in, and sitting at a table were two eighty-something women in short-sleeved housecoats, drinking coffee and listening to music.

"Honey, just set those down here," said the woman to my left.

I set my basket down on the floor and leaned over to take out their meals. I cautioned them about the sweet potatoes wrapped in tin foil.

"They're still pretty warm. Be careful when you pick them up."

"Do you see that cleavage, Marge?" said the woman across from me.

I was wearing a grey t-shirt and a thin white jacket. It's been unusually warm, so a winter coat wasn't needed. My shirt wasn't low cut by any means, but apparently when I leaned over, my Canal of Cleavage was front and center.

"Make sure you're not leaning over when you deliver meals to men!" the women advised. Embarrassed, I smiled and said I'd be careful.

On our last visit, the instruction on the clipboard was to call the client, who was in a wheelchair and lived in a third-floor apartment of an old house. He would then throw down the keys to the front door from the window that opened up to the fire escape. Deacon said there was another way and asked if I would be OK climbing the fire escape instead. While he parked the car, I eyed the steep and narrow stairs that led to the client's apartment. They reminded me of the steps outside the apartment I lived in when I weighed three hundred pounds.

I thought about it for a second, then called the client and said, "I'll climb up your fire escape in a minute."

I got out of Deacon's car with my basket and saw the client open the window. Three-hundred-pound me hated climbing my apartment steps all those years ago, but without much choice at this point, I grabbed the handrail and started my ascent.

I got to the top without any issues and without losing my breath. I looked to make sure no cleavage had made its way out on my way up. I handed the client his meal and cautioned him about the sweet potato. He smiled and thanked me. I turned around and took in the view. From that vantage point I could see the Tower of Learning at the University of Pittsburgh, and further on, the tops of a few of the taller buildings downtown. It was quite a sight. When my three-year-old grandson accomplishes something, he exclaims, "I did dit!" As I walked down the fire escape, I high-fived my former three-hundred-pound self. I did "dit."

When I was losing weight and started to exercise, I was focused on big goals, like competitive walking and days-long bike trips. The fire escape made me realize that I've taken for granted those fleeting moments of movement, like taking the stairs rather than the elevator, walking the dog around the block, or standing for an hour or more. I'd lost sight of the everyday activities that hurt before but don't anymore.

How cool is it to change the way you eat and move for no other reason than to climb stairs without feeling depleted? What an honorable goal!

I admire people who want to climb mountains and run for hours. But if you can climb stairs and walk around the block again? Man, you did "dit."

Flawed and … Inspiring?
Posted June 2012

In October 2007, I had the good fortune of meeting a complicated, humble, and inspirational man named David, who was sexually molested as a child and lost his mother when he was seventeen. Yet, at six hundred fifty pounds, David found the courage to lose four hundred pounds, and he told his story to the world. David and I met when we were on *Oprah*, and he went on to do many other TV appearances, including the TLC documentary, *650-Pound Virgin*.

David has been out of the spotlight for a few years, but he resurfaced on the *Today* show Wednesday, having gained three hundred pounds. Below is an excerpt of his sad, yet very honest, truth from a *Huffington Post* article: "'All my life I was this monster in my head, and all of a sudden to be this good looking guy, it blew my mind away. I didn't know how to deal with it.' Smith also felt like "a terrible mess" on the inside, and eventually turned to alcohol and drugs to cope.

"When those outlets didn't help, he turned once again to food. 'A lot of people were counting on me to be inspiring, and I didn't want to let anybody down. But I just felt so bad, I didn't know how to cope,' he says."

Weight doesn't disappear. It hides, waiting for you to feed it your fear. Seeing David again put me face-to-face with my own twenty-pound gain and the one hundred fifty other pounds lurking in the dark recesses of my mind.

I've searched (though not as desperately as I think I have) for a reason for my gain, for something outside of me that I can blame. But the truth lies not in what I eat or my reluctance to move or the pain of arthritis or the mood swings of perimenopause. The truth is deep inside me, buried in mistrust, and David's truth has nudged me to at least admit that lately I've been walking, zombie-like, down the path I swerved to avoid seven years ago when I started losing weight. Major conflict and heartache have come into my life and I can't sort through it all like laundry. I look longingly back, like Lot's wife, at the weight-loss path I diligently walked for years and I turned into a twenty-pound pillar of salt, with the very real potential of adding one hundred fifty more.

Losing weight and, more importantly, keeping it off, takes a lot of concentration. Distractions, however, deactivate concentration, and when it comes to weight loss and maintenance, the distractions that deactivate concentration aren't simple things like the lure of an ice cream cone on a hot summer day. They are deep-seated emotional issues or family issues or work issues that not only distract, but cause us to react in a way that is counter to what our concentrated self would "approve" of: mindless eating, drinking, not caring.

David didn't consciously gain back three hundred pounds. Nothing in him said, "I want to be morbidly obese again." I didn't consciously gain twenty pounds. And nothing in my mind is saying, "I want to be three hundred pounds again."

A lot of people were counting on me to be inspiring…

I want to inspire, but I'm as vulnerable and flawed as anyone on this path, including David. And that truth by itself is inspiring.

I wish David all the love and self-care he can find as he works through his "terrible mess," and I hope he finds the truth that lies beneath, the one I could see in his smile and in his eyes when I met him: kindness, sincerity, and a strong desire to live.

Throwing Out The Three-Hundred-Pound Pitch
Posted January 2013

During an interview in 2008, *Talk of the Nation* host Neal Conan asked Carrie Fisher why she wrote *Wishful Drinking*, a memoir about her experience with manic depression, addiction, and electroconvulsive therapy (ECT), particularly given its stigma. She answered: "The thing about telling it is, if I make it a secret, it has enormous power. Then I have to be scared. 'Will they find out?' And I'm, like, 'If you find it out about me, I've already got there first, so you're gonna hear my version.'"

Google my name and it's easy to find me and my three-hundred-pound truth. I put it out there willingly in 2005, hoping to find kindred spirits, people who were on a path of embracing their own truth about weight. With more than one and a half million page hits on my blog in eight years, clearly there are more than a few of us seeking that truth.

I don't mind telling you I weighed three hundred pounds. You get it. It's not so easy telling someone you've only recently met and you're on a first date. You order a salad and he orders wings with blue cheese dressing and he jokingly says, "New Year's resolution?" and you say, "Well, kind of."

The story of me isn't an easy story to digest. It's one thing to say, "I weighed three hundred pounds seven years ago." It's quite another to say, "My weight impacts my life every day." Some women seek tall, dark, and handsome. Me? I seek someone who won't eat Doritos in front of me.

In Pittsburgh we call it "nebbing" when you want to find out about someone. I have one of the nebbiest neighbors ever. A small, balding old man, he's forever watching my house. There isn't a light I turn on or off that he doesn't know about. He's harmless enough, but it's a little unnerving having your every move observed.

That's kind of how it feels when I meet someone new and they find out my name. They're going to neb. Heck, I do it! But I prefer he hear my weighty truth from my lips and not from a photo of three-hundred-pound me in a purple dress contrasted with the me he has just met. Yes, my blog is my truth and my voice, but for someone who isn't accustomed to reading weight loss blogs, my blog can be a lot of truth to take in without some advance warning.

While I don't consider obesity a character flaw, many in this world do, especially the Judgy McJudgers who tease, roll their eyes, and all out hate on fat people. Because I was obese, there's an added chance of judgment that I take into consideration when the "So, tell me about yourself" convo starts.

A few years ago, I met someone who, after a few dates, asked me straight up about loose skin. "Do you have any?" was his exact question. My response? "You'll never find out," and I kicked him out.

Now while that sounds all bold and "Go me!" it was embarrassing, and I wondered how many other men would be wondering the same thing.

Not long after that date, I met someone else, and we dated for eighteen months. My truth became a part of our relationship, an almost non-entity, and he didn't eat Doritos in front of me, either. Now that I'm single again, my choices are either to stay in and hide or to get out there and try. I choose to try. After all, I was who I was and I am who I am, and the next guy up to bat has a number of options of what to do with that curve ball. If it's to inquire about loose skin, then he isn't worthy. If it's to stick around, then I'll explain the part about the Doritos.

Pulling Back the Sheets: Intimacy and Body Image
Posted June 2013

My two-year-old granddaughter Mae loves to be naked. She'll strip down whenever the mood strikes and run around the house yelling, "Nakee! Nakee!"

"Nakee" and alone, I'm better than I used to be. For the most part, I accept (or at least live with or just ignore) the sags, bags, wrinkles, and rolls.

"Nakee" and not alone? Let's just say I'm not as comfortable as Mae.

No matter our body size, intimacy and body image is something many of us deal with on some level. We can wear clothes that flatter, cover, disguise, hide, tuck in, suck in, boost, and separate. But stripped down, bare and naked, the truth is beheld by a beholder, and for those of us with body issues, trust is critical. Trust that when we are told that our bodies are beautiful *just as they are*, the person saying it believes it.

At my goal weight six years ago, I was at a picnic with my then-husband. A male neighbor asked him what it was like to be with a "completely different woman" in bed. Without missing a beat, my husband said, "She's the same beautiful woman I've always known."

I was disgusted by the man's question, but I was more surprised by my reaction to my husband's response. He had always told me I was beautiful, no matter what I weighed. He loved me through thick and thin. But it was at that moment that I realized that I never trusted him or any man's words of beauty and admiration *in the realm of intimacy*. Why? Because to me, I was not beautiful, not in bed anyway. And if my truth was that my body was not beautiful, then, in my mind, that was *every partner's* truth, despite what they said to the contrary.

My sexual repertoire, at all my weights, has included remaining semi-clothed or having sheets or blankets strategically wrapped around me, and employing carefully choreographed maneuvers to keep body parts from being exposed or displayed in unflattering ways. This routine was born from years of negative self-dialogue and a subconscious buy-in to the impossible societal definitions of beauty and sex. My belief that my body, in its natural state, is best enjoyed covered up and not in the open is so deeply ingrained that it is as much a part of my identity as my blue eyes.

Since starting a meditation practice several years ago, my mind has been on a journey of truth. Emotions I thought I had under wraps sometimes swim to the surface and demand to be felt at seemingly inopportune moments. Trying to stop them is like telling a swimmer to keep holding her breath when she comes up for air.

The most powerful undercover moment to date happened a few months ago when I was with my boyfriend Jim. All he did was whisper, "You're beautiful," and *in that moment*, what I thought and felt down to my very core was, 'Wow, he has really bad taste in women. I'm so gross, can't he *see* that?'

It was such an overwhelmingly sad and empty feeling, it made me cry. Words tumbled out of my mouth as I told him about my life-long struggle to accept my body. He stroked my hair and, when I calmed down, he simply said, "I know. I see you struggle with it every time we're together. But I think you're beautiful."

And here I thought no one noticed my strategic maneuvers.

Sex, especially in middle age, isn't discussed much out in the open, namely because anyone (usually a woman) who reveals they enjoy sex at all, especially those of us who are not married, is subject to criticism from any number of ideological know-it-alls. Body image can affect our lives in ways we aren't always consciously aware of, including — and perhaps most notably — our sex lives. How can we hear, believe, trust, and accept another's truth about our bodies when our own view of our bodies is less than stellar or even polar opposite of our beholder's? How do we pull back the sheet, even a little, and welcome their truth, and meet intimacy with no body image barriers?

I doubt I'll ever be as carefree naked as my granddaughter, but I promised Jim I would trust him and believe his truth about my body. He knows this is a leap of faith for me, but it's one that will hopefully pay off with a deeper connection between the sheets...or above the sheets with the lights on.

Vulnerable
Posted September 2013

I've been listening to the audio version of Brené Brown's book, *Daring Greatly*, for the last few weeks. Halfway through the seven-disc book, I knew I had to have a hard copy. *Daring Greatly* is a book that screams, "Write in my margins, people! Highlight! Underline! Reread!"

Embracing vulnerability is a new concept for me. My MO is usually to ignore/avoid/run away, especially among people who could, and sometimes did, judge me based on my appearance. But there was one time when I didn't let vulnerability win. It was on a May day in 2001 when I gave out the Tony Fabri Memorial Scholarships at the Clarion High School auditorium in front of hundreds of teenagers, who, in my imagination, could be the worst audience of all when you're feeling vulnerable. But Tony was best friends with my daughters and many others, and I loved him like a son. When he died, an entire community went into mourning, and my daughters' lives changed forever.

When Tony's parents asked me to present the scholarship awards, I was both honored and scared to death. But I kept in perspective what they were asking me to do: honor their son. They also asked if it would be OK if someone videotaped my presentation because they couldn't bring themselves to attend. I didn't hesitate to consent. I have a Ph.D. in grief. I know how caring for yourself while grieving means sometimes not touching the hot spots. Wait until they cool a bit, then lay your hands on them.

I don't mind public speaking when I'm prepared. Throw me out in front of a crowd with little or no warning and ask me to say something intelligent? I'm pretty sure I'd rather pass a kidney stone. But that day, I was more than prepared. I was eager to talk about Tony and the legacy of his short-lived life. Only a few times did I think about what people thought of my weight.

What I'm realizing as I read *Daring Greatly* is that vulnerability is there, up front or in the background, from the moment I wake up until the moment I fall asleep. Yesterday I went to my first-ever aqua aerobics class. Not only would I be trying something new, I would be wearing a bathing suit in front of a dozen or more people!

As I should have predicted, but didn't trust, was that the outcome of my first experience with aqua aerobics was the same as when I plow through most of my other vulnerable moments. It was worth it, I had fun, and I met other body types wearing bathing suits in public without care. I also changed my attitude about aqua aerobics being easy (my arm muscles are complaining this morning), and I walked from the pool to the locker room with a little more belief in myself and with a little more love in my heart for who I am: vulnerable and imperfect, but usually hopeful.

I'm learning that being my own best friend is about opening up and being receptive to vulnerability, rather than caving in to my self-nemesis who, in the face of a challenge, yells in my ear, "Oh please, please, *please* can we not think about this? Can we just pop popcorn and eat

Hershey Kisses and watch the first season of *Mad Men* for the third time? Please!?"

Every day we're "out there," whether we leave our homes or not. (The Internet is a breeding ground for vulnerability!) Vulnerability is present when we start a new job, go out on a first date, break up with someone, get fired, or go to the doctor. Heck, vulnerability is present in a restaurant! I always feel bothersome when I ask a server, "Can you please hold the capers and bacon and add a few more tomatoes instead? Oh, and can I get the dressing on the side?"

Online or in person, our faces, our bodies, our personalities, our cars, our houses, our coffee order at Starbucks, our sandwich order at Sheetz, and even the books our children and grandchildren want to check out from the library make a statement about who we are, and in those moments, we're open to judgment by the outside and the inside. That's right. We judge our own vulnerabilities!

I know that many of you have already figured this out, but wow, clarity is creeping up on me like the spider that walked up my calf on Saturday as I scrubbed floors. Not wanting to kill it, I let it creep while I walked outside and set it free, all the while fighting the urge to sweep him away like he wasn't real. Sort of like the times when I feel most vulnerable and I want to crawl in a hole and shut my eyes and hope no one wants anything from me.

My audio copy of *Daring Greatly* is due back at my library on Friday (as is the book my grandson checked out, *Captain Underpants and the Preposterous Plight of the Purple Potty*). While I now own a hard copy, I was hoping to finish the book on CD. When I tried to renew it online, I couldn't because someone else has reserved it. That's OK. It's comforting to know I'm not the only one trying to stop the freight train of vulnerability and throw it in reverse.

Common Ground

Adventures in Maintenance: Letters to Santa*
Posted December 2013

* From 2012 to 2014, four other weight-loss bloggers and I formed a group, Adventures in Maintenance, *to address issues facing people in weight maintenance. We published a post on the same topic on the first Monday of each month.*

How lucky am I to have run into Santa last week at the drug store! He was waiting for a prescription ("Just a little something to keep me awake on Christmas Eve!" he said) and trying to take his blood pressure. I told him I was in the middle of writing him a letter. He said if I helped him figure out how to use the "dang machine" (because Mrs. Claus was always worried about his blood pressure this time of year), that I could just tell him what I wanted for Christmas. Easy enough, and it saved me a stamp. I got his forearm in the cuff, pushed a few buttons, and in less than a minute, Santa had his numbers: 120/80.

"Not bad for a guy your age," I said.

"The Mrs. will be pleased," he said. "Now, what can I do for you, Lynnie? Have you been a good girl this year?"

"Well, I've been a, well, hmmmm. Let's just say I've not been the most stellar maintainer this year. I've made some bad choices. But it doesn't make me a bad person, right? I mean, you won't put eggplant in my stocking, will you? You know I hate eggplant."

"Ho ho ho! Of course not! What *do* you want for Christmas?"

"I want that spark back, Santa. That determination, you know? I seemed to have lost it this year."

"Hmmm...Tell me, what's different this year?"

"You see, I met someone. Someone who likes to cook soufflés and eggs Benedict. Someone who likes Italian food and eating at four- and five-star restaurants."

"Ho ho ho! Is he force-feeding you ravioli?"

"No! No! It's just so tempting and I love food and I lose my mind sometimes and…. Why are you rolling your eyes?"

"Lynnie, Lynnie, Lynnie. You of all people should know an excuse when you see one. You have demonstrated restraint in the past, right? Seems to me you need to take the gag off your inner voice."

"My inner voice?"

"Don't you remember? You used to ask yourself: 'How will I feel five minutes after I eat this?'"

"That's right! I forgot about that."

"And how's that Y membership working out? I understand you couldn't bike much this summer, but are you still hiking?"

"Um…well, you know. It's gotten cold and…"

"What the…? Didn't you grow up in Minnesota?"

"Well, yes…"

"You lived in that white house in the middle of the block between Dreesen's and Mrs. Stoltenberg. You played outside all the time in the snow! And you walked, all bundled up in your snowsuit and snowmobile boots, to school…uphill both ways, I recall…and to work at your dad's store."

"Yes, well, but I'm older now and my body doesn't work the way it used to. I need new knees, my shoulders are shot…Again with the eyeroll!"

"Again with the excuses."

"I know," I sighed. "I just have no motivation."

"Motivation, snowtivation. Body over mind, girl. You know that. I've read your blog. You used to preach it all the time. You just do it. You get out there and *move*! You like the pool, right?"

"Yes."

"Go back! Stop throwing away thirty-five dollars a month!"

"Money *can* be motivating. I don't suppose there will be some of that under my tree this year?"

"Ho ho ho! No."

"Can't blame a girl for trying."

"But speaking of money, I understand you've signed up to walk a 5K next weekend to raise money for arthritis research."

"That's right, I did! The Jingle Bell Walk/Run. Crap! What was I thinking? I'm afraid I won't be able to walk it in the time I've challenged myself to. I used to walk 5Ks in thirty-eight minutes…"

"Used to. That was then. Now you won't walk it in thirty-eight minutes. So what! What's wrong with, oh, say, forty-five minutes? Or fifty? Or even an hour? It's your effort and dedication to a cause that is most important, not beating up your body to chase after some ghost of the past."

"You're right. I just…"

"Just what? Let go, Lynnie. Live now. Today. One meal at a time. One workout at a time."

"You're right."

"I'm always right! Except when Mrs. Claus tells me I'm not. Now off my lap with you! Be good, Lynnie, and don't forget to leave me some cookies and milk!"

"How about a soufflé?"

"Even better! Merry Christmas, Lynnie!"

"Merry Christmas, Santa. And thanks."

"No need to thank me. Just help me get my arm out of this cuff!"

Lessons Learned from a Three-Legged Cat
Posted December 2013

Three weeks ago, my boyfriend Jim adopted a three-legged cat. He had no name.

Cat was the pet of a man who recently passed away. The man's daughter, who took in Cat when her father died, already had three cats, two dogs, several mice, a couple of birds, and a ferret. She loved the cat, but simply didn't have room for another pet. A vet tech, who knew of her situation and was familiar with Jim's soft spot for all cats, feral and domestic, called him to ask if he'd consider adopting the four-year-old.

Details are sketchy of Cat's life prior to living with the man who passed away. Cat lost his leg, the vet tech said, in a fight with a wild animal. Cat's ears are also chewed up a bit. She said that prior to living with the man, Cat was also teased and possibly tortured by a group of young men who lived in a university dorm.

Always on the side of the underdog, Jim agreed to adopt Cat. When the daughter and Cat arrived, Cat was *not* happy in the too-small carrier. She released him, and—before we could even get a good look at him—he ran under our bed. For only having three legs, Cat is fast! For three days, nothing Jim or I did would convince him to come out while we were awake. He ate and used the litter box while we slept.

On day three of his self-imposed exile, I was in my office next to the bedroom when Cat wandered out and stared at me from the doorway. I said hello. He stared at me for a few minutes. I slowly got up from my chair and he bolted back under the bed.

The next night, I walked out of the bathroom after brushing my teeth and found Cat sitting in the hallway. This time, he didn't run away, even when I slowly sat down on the floor about three feet away. I softly talked to him, and he cautiously walked over to me, purring. I reached out my hand. He cowered, but held his ground. I touched the top of his head and he moved to rub his neck against my hand. When I stood up to go to bed, he walked—not bolted—to the rug under the bed.

Fast forward three weeks. Cat, now known as Tres, is still a little skittish, but he's all about being around Jim and me. He walks between our legs when we're getting dressed, plays with his mouse toy in the living room while we watch TV, and eats his food when we're in the kitchen.

It's clear that Tres loves love. No wild animal and no cruel humans squelched his hope or desire to be cared for. Tres has me thinking about how we all need to feel safe and to be acknowledged for the unique individuals we are. But it's often fear and what's unique about us that keeps us hiding under the bed.

I've felt a nagging fear in the back of my mind ever since I wrote about my imaginary encounter with Santa. I'd written that I was worried that I wouldn't complete the Jingle Bell 5K walk in the time that I could have completed a 5K a few years ago. Santa, of course, told me that time didn't matter, that commitment to the cause of raising money for arthritis research was what was really important. But it's hard to take advice from Santa when I'm the one writing Santa's dialogue, you know?

In the car today, I turned off the radio and concentrated on the nagging, the dread, the fear. What was I afraid of? After several miles of driving, I identified it as fear of pain and fear of not being able to keep up with people who walked without a limp, especially the people who would be walking with me: my daughter Carlene, Jim, and my granddaughter Claire. Daughter Cassie will run the 5k, and I realized that I've been comparing myself to her, too. I felt like Tres when he first moved in with us: skittish, hiding under the bed, and feeling out of his element.

Then I thought about Tres and the trust he's built for Jim and me these last few weeks. Tres doesn't intellectually understand the concept of trust and love, but clearly it's innate. He doesn't feel he has anything to prove to us. He doesn't care that he has three legs.

I, too, have nothing to prove to the people who love me. I have to do nothing more than be myself. Walk what I can in the time that I can. Pain will ensue, but it's nothing I can't handle. Limp? Yup. It's how I walk anymore. And, come on now, Lynn, it's a walk for arthritis research! There will be people there with far more disability than me. People who will no doubt humble and inspire me.

My fear is in my head, created on the premise of "What if?"

I can do this, whatever "this" turns out to be. And when I see Tres again, I will give him a few extra pets and thank him for showing me a side of trust and love I haven't experienced in a long time.

Own It!
Posted April 2014

Jim and I had coffee at Starbucks a few weeks ago with our friends Dave and Peg. The manager came around with samples of Starbucks' new bakery items: chocolate croissants, berry something or others, and coffee cake. The guys dug in, but Peg and I refused them. I said to Peg that I've gained a few pounds since meeting Jim, to which Jim said, "I may have had a hand in that."

While I appreciate Jim's willingness to shoulder some of the responsibility, absolutely no one but me decides what I eat. He's off the hook.

Jim is a capital "F" Foodie. He's a great cook and loves to go out for dinner. He understands my desire to eat clean and doesn't push food on me. But his way of life has influenced me, and what I've seen happen in fifteen months is exactly what fellow blogger Shelley described in a recent post: "I have slowly let other things become more of the norm instead of the exception."

While writing this post, I noticed how often I wanted to use the words "blame" and "fault." I'd originally written, "Jim was willing to take part of the blame, but it was my fault." Eww! Where's the loving kindness in that? Nowhere, that's where. Losing and maintaining weight takes determination and vigilance, absolutely. But it also takes a kind approach to disappointment, not blaming, shaming, and faulting.

Have I let more food exceptions become the norm? Yes. Am I disappointed with some of my choices? Yes. But I've been disappointed in some choices my children have made over the years and I still love them. If I've learned nothing else in my fifty years, it's that I respond more positively to identifying a feeling as disappointing than I do blaming and faulting myself. Blaming someone else takes the responsibility off me, and blaming myself is punishment. I cannot grow or learn from either of these reactions. Disappointment, on the other hand, allows for self-examination and spurs me to do better, to make amends.

Our friends' and family's food behaviors can have sway in our lives. But our friends and family are not responsible for our choices.

Jim is an adventurous foodie, and if I choose to eat something he offers, that's solely my decision. Now, whether I'm listening to my inner voice at the time, that, too, is up to me. Like last night's pound cake incident while we watched a hockey game.

Jim: "Want some?"
Inner Voice: "You've been on track all day! Atta girl! Keep it up!"
Me: "No, thank you!"
Jim: "Oh, man! Did you see that shot?"
My decision to not eat pound cake had no impact on Jim's life.

I've been at this online weight-loss/weight-maintenance blogging thing for almost nine years. One of the things I hear the most from people who read my blog is the angst they feel about other people's food behaviors, either in the form of "pushing" food on them or not accepting their decision to improve their food choices; food as a form of psychological pressure. I know much has been written about this issue, but it comes down to individual choice. My food choices are not responsible for someone else's happiness. Nor is any resulting weight gain or weight loss or weight neutrality a result of something someone else has done, said, made, or offered.

I sound militant, but losing weight and maintaining weight takes a bit of militancy. Militancy based in loving kindness for one's own body. It's yours! The only one you'll ever have! Own it.

Disappointment happens. Let go of the blame and shame and fault. And don't let anyone tell you what you should or shouldn't eat.

Boom. Done.
Posted May 2014

I'm not a very good painter, as in painter of walls and furniture. I've had ambition to paint, but never enough to get me through an entire project, or at least an entire project done well.

I can see the potential in a worn piece of furniture, and I can imagine what a room would look like painted a different color. But until this week, I didn't bother to do the one thing I needed to do to complete a painting project successfully: Learn how.

My niece is moving here for the summer. I have a spare room and a spare bed, and instead of hauling her dresser out here from Minnesota, I told her I'd get one.

I looked for a new dresser in my price range. It doesn't exist. So I sent out an email to local friends and family members to keep an eye out for a used dresser. Jim's mom called and said a friend of hers was moving to Florida and was getting rid of all her furniture. Perfect! For twenty bucks, I got a five-drawer, 1950s-style chest of drawers, and man, was it ugly! But I saw its potential. A little paint and it would look great!

The blessing and curse of dating a carpenter is that I can't fake my lack of carpentry knowledge. The blessing is that I can plead ignorance when it comes to things I know I can't do, like fix the exhaust fan in the bathroom. The curse is when I think I can do something and I screw it up.

In my mind, the dresser project was going to go this way:
1. Pick out and buy paint, both a main color and an accent color.
2. Buy a brush.
3. Throw down a drop cloth.
4. Paint.
5. Boom. Done.

In Jim's mind, the dresser project was going to go this way:
1. Ask the guy at the paint store what he recommended I do to the dresser to get it ready for the paint. *Sandpaper? What?*
2. Ask the guy at the paint store to recommend the right kind of primer. *Primer?*
3. Ask the guy at the paint store to recommend the right kind of base paint. *You mean there is more than one kind?*
4. Buy a block of medium sandpaper.
5. Buy a four-inch roller and a couple of pads.
6. Remove handles of the dresser.
7. Scuff dresser.
8. Prime dresser.
9. Wait at least four hours. *Those are the instructions? Where? On the can?*
10. Paint dresser.
11. Wait another four hours. *This will take forEVER!*
12. Paint dresser again.
13. Next day *(Next day?)*, prepare area for accent color by taping the edges of the bevels.
14. Paint accent color.

15. Wait four hours. *Tapping foot…*
16. Paint accent color again.
17. Dry overnight before reassembling. *Is that another gray hair?*
18. Boom. Done.

No wonder my painting projects never turn out the way I envision. You know where this is going, don't you?

The reason so many of us don't lose weight or don't keep it off is that we never take the time to learn how. It should be easy, right? You stop eating so much, you move around a little more. Boom. Done.

But it's not that easy. There's way more to it than that. You can be excited that you bought the right paint, feel smart that you bought the right roller, and pat yourself on the back for selecting the right drop cloth, but the dresser won't paint itself.

Boom/done doesn't happen in weight loss, weight maintenance, or any goal we choose to pursue. As my fortune cookie reminded me last week, "Success is a planned event." Success has many definitions and criteria, but however you define it, success requires a commitment—every day—to patience, adaptability, and the willingness to learn.

Weight-Loss Dropout
Posted January 2018

Many of you "met" me years ago through my Lynn's Weigh blog, the space where I wrote about (mostly) weight and all the issues surrounding it (the good, the bad, the recipes, the exercise). I believed then, as I do now, that there is no easy fix for the physical and emotional complexities of weight, both gaining and losing.

I also believed, and I don't anymore, that I would always be in control of my physical and emotional world if I regularly (obsessively?) did

ABC. In doing so, I would maintain the results I'd worked so hard for: a (too) thin body and the (faux) happiness that it brings. I believed I had to be a certain way — the Lynn's Weigh — in order to have a voice on the subject of weight. When menopause, the crippling effects of arthritis, and the weight gain started four years ago, I felt I'd let everyone down — my readers, my children, my boyfriend, my doctors (some of whom keep the *People* magazine in my folder to inspire other patients). But mostly, I felt like I'd let myself down.

In two years, since absorbing Lynn's Weigh into my Zen Bag Lady blog, I've been quietly trying to make peace with my physical and emotional changes without laying blame, feeling guilty, or being angry and frustrated.

The results? I fail miserably sometimes on all points. But I don't fail all the time. In fact, I fail less today than I did a month, six months, and a year ago. In widening my field of vision, I was supported by and found comfort in the words of former weight-loss bloggers Jeannette Fulda and Shauna Reid, both of whom wrote pieces in 2017 that resonated with me.

Jeannette wrote: "These days the Internet seems like a much more misogynistic, judgmental place, like a flood of tourists have swarmed the local bar and you never know what asshole is going to show up, start a fight and then breeze off, never to be seen again."

We see this all the time everywhere now, way more than when we started blogging in the 2000s. Some people have no filter, no compassion, and no common sense. Words hurt, especially mean and hurtful words that come from some anonymous little puke hiding behind a computer screen. People say to ignore it, but I'm not emotionally built that way. I welcome constructive criticism that comes from a place of love and concern, but it takes me an inordinate amount of time to unfeel the pain of hurtful and untrue words. While I didn't have many trolls on Lynn's Weigh and, so far, none on Zen Bag Lady, "coming out" like this, with the (not so surprising) revelation that I'm not the same person I was two, eight, or thirteen years ago, might cause some people to gloat or to throw my words in my face. But I'm going to take that risk because speaking up for change rather than staying silent and hidden is worth it. As Jeannette reminded me and everyone else, "People have the right to change."

Indeed.

Shauna wrote: "What I struggle with is contradictory. First there are the feelings of failure for not remaining the After photo, like that invalidates any value of the book (*The Amazing Adventures of Dietgirl*) entirely. I wrote about the After photo struggles on my blog for a while, then slinked away from the topic. I avoided people and places. There's been so much shame and fraudy feels…Then there is the part of me that is so bloody done hiding and ready to make peace with it all."

Amen!

Sometimes I look at my After photos with a bit of regret, but I don't regret the journey one bit. Like Shauna and Jeannette, I hope my words helped people on their own journeys. Gaining weight has been humbling, especially given the myriad physical shitstorm that's been my life the last several years. But looking at the Afters also reminds me that nothing is permanent.

I don't owe the Internet an apology, but I want to continue the conversation with all of you in this different chapter of my (and your!) life. You're not the same folks you were two, eight, or thirteen years ago, either, right?

Thanks for being here. Namaste.

Common Ground

What's Real, What's True, What's On Repeat?
Posted August 2019

I buy it with good intentions, but good intentions don't preserve lettuce. It usually dies in my refrigerator crisper.

For years I ate a salad almost every day. Every. Day. Trust me, if you do that—or eat anything every day (except maybe chocolate, cheese, and bread)—you'll get bored.

I ate salad almost every day because I told myself it was good for me, and physically speaking, it is good when you consider salad at its basic nutritional level, sans all the stuff that makes it really good like croutons and ranch dressing, or if you're in western Pennsylvania, French fries. But I also ate a salad almost every day because I told myself that if I didn't put salad on repeat, I would gain a whole bunch of weight and show the world what an impulsive, undisciplined person I was.

Because of other people. Yeah…that's a reason to eat salad every day.

What is real and what we tell ourselves is real are often different things, and often are not true. Undergirding what we think is real is usually fear, which is not fun to admit, let alone deal with. It's easier to blame circumstances or other people for our actions, reactions, and go-to coping mechanisms. In the case of eating salad every day, what was real had nothing to do with outward appearances and everything to do with my fear of losing control of my body, and then if (and I did) gain weight, having to love myself as I am, and then living inside that loved body in public (and in private).

I'm better with the whole loving-my-body-as-it-is, and I won't go back to eating a salad every day in support of what I know now isn't real or true, but sometimes I still act from within that false reality of "If I eat a salad, I am (somehow) a better person."

Weight is an easy target. But often our feelings about our weight masks more wide spread beliefs of what we inherently believe is real but not true.

Buddhist psychologist Tara Brach talks of this often. There is so much false reality in the world, our respective countries, our backyards, and our lives. Individually and collectively, when we cling to and act on what we think is real—whether it's our political, religious, or medical beliefs (I'm referring specifically to vaccinations), or ideas and opinions of other people based on their race, sexual orientation, or gender identification—we expose our fears. For instance, it is not possible to hate or even casually disregard someone who doesn't pray or look like you, or to take advantage of or purposely hurt someone without being afraid, to the core, of losing something, be it self or national identity, power, or fate (either here or after death).

What does this have to do with eating a salad? There is so much injustice all around, from the self-inflicted and personal to the universal. I am in the world, and so are you. Our personal concerns and belief systems, no matter how big or small, mingle and coalesce with the world, and they affect the world in a micro and macro way. It makes sense, and is necessary, to take a personal inventory and contemplate what we think is real to discover if it merely supports an ideology born of fear or if it is true.

Here's an example, something I experienced and wrote in my personal journal prior to my hip replacement a few months ago:

"I woke up this morning feeling deeply sad and frustrated. I'd had a horrible dream and it took me a few minutes after I woke up to realize it wasn't real. It set the tone for the morning.

"After breakfast, I put laundry in the wash, loaded dishes in the dishwasher, and started vacuuming. My left hip kept threatening to toss me on the floor with every step. When I needed to change attachments to vacuum the bathroom floor, I couldn't disconnect one of the hoses. I tried, failed, and cursed, tried, failed, and cursed before I threw myself against the wall and cried. I thought I was crying because I couldn't change the hose and because my hip hurt, but they were just the catalyst. In and of themselves, hip pain and vacuum attachment failures wouldn't make me cry. Make me angry, yes. But I felt empty, and an even larger emptiness rose up; an indescribable loneliness.

"I took a deep breath and did a brief inquiry, ala my years of meditation training, and I think I figured out that I was crying because I couldn't stop thinking about how last night I witnessed a tender moment between an adult daughter and her mother. A simple thing, really. The daughter and mother were talking and laughing with each other in that familiar way parents and children do when they like each other as people and love each other as family. It's an intimacy that the outside world isn't meant to understand or intrude upon. As I cried, I realized that what was really true in my head and causing the tears was not the hip pain and the vacuum snafu. That stuff was real. What was true was I missed my daughters and was frustrated that I didn't live closer, and—and this is the hardest one to admit—sad that I didn't have that same kind of intimacy with my own mother."

Parsing that out was hard, but in the end it was worth it. The things I put on repeat—the "you shoulds," the "how could yous," the "WTF were you thinkings," the "why are you crying now???"—deserve my attention! And your own WTFs deserve your thinking, too.

Take inventory. Ask yourself: What is real? What is true? What do I put on repeat?

The world feels like it's turned upside down, and there are times when getting inside myself seems selfish. But if we don't get inside ourselves and figure it out, who will? No one, that's who.

Now go eat a salad. Or not. All I ask is that you question why you do what you do on repeat when it feels…wonky.

Lynn Haraldson

The Fine Line Between Compliment and Judgement
Posted February 2020

In all the years I've written about weight issues, I've never addressed the "compliment." I thought I had, but I checked my blog archives and, nope, not a word. It was a conversation I had only in my head.

It's been a while since I've written about weight issues, mostly because weight lives more in the periphery than the forefront of my life these days. It's still there. I can see it. But lately I'm more concerned about crossing my legs before I sneeze than what I weigh.

I'm bringing weight back into the conversation because of a recent meeting with a friend I haven't seen in many months. When she got out of her car, she was notably thinner. I didn't say anything about it. Instead, I complimented the necklace she was wearing, a lovely triple circle diamond pendant. She said she bought it for herself as a reward for losing weight. She explained that at her last doctor's visit, her blood pressure was up and she wanted to try to control it through diet and exercise. Considering she is fifty-nine years old and post-menopausal, that's no small feat, so extra kudos to her for her success.

I didn't want to say anything about her obvious weight loss for a few reasons, one being that if she lost weight because she's sick, that is her story to tell and not my business to neb. The other reason is that I'm careful offering "compliments" regarding any changes I notice about someone's physical appearance, particularly when it's clear(ish) that they've lost weight. It's usually without malicious intent that someone says, "You look great! Have you lost weight?" But often what the recipient hears (or at least internalizes) is, "You weren't good enough before."

In recent years, people like Lizzo, Kelly Clarkson, Chrissy Metz, and Rebel Wilson have shut down weight critics, but they also admit that the comments hurt sometimes. And their body acceptance doesn't mean that everyone's lovin' on their own bodies all of a sudden, either. How someone looks still equals approval. Everything we wear (or don't wear), what we put on our face, the way we age, what we look like, and especially what we weigh is important to someone other than ourselves, often people closest to us, even though it's none of their business.

One example I will remember forever happened while planning my daughter Cassie's wedding in 2006 when I was actively losing weight. I was looking for someone to make cupcakes and a small wedding cake and several friends recommended a woman who had a small baking business in her home. I made an appointment and went to talk to her.

She'd never met me so of course had no idea I once weighed more than three hundred pounds. At the time I met her, I weighed about one hundred seventy pounds, and if it was the first time you had ever seen me, the thought might cross your mind that I was overweight. We sat down at her dining room table — the woman, me, and the woman's twenty-something daughter, whose leg was in a large metal brace.

After some brief chit-chat, and apropos of absolutely nothing, the woman outright apologized to me for her daughter's weight. I was speechless, and the poor girl looked mortified. The girl launched into an explanation (read: she was apologizing, too) about how she used to be on some high school sports team when she was in a horrific accident that crushed her leg. Subsequently, she spent months in rehab and, apparently, gaining weight. Her mother then said — and I'm sure you can guess what's coming — "She has such a pretty face, doesn't she? If only..." and at that moment, I thought I was going to lose my shit all over her unforgivable parenting ass, but I didn't. I just smiled at the girl and told her how sorry I was. I didn't get specific.

So what does this have to do with complimenting someone who has lost weight? Everything. Anytime we comment on someone's weight, we're making a judgement, even if we mean it in the most sincere, kind way. I know some of you might think it would be rude to ignore the obvious, and really, who doesn't want to compliment a friend? I get that, and I've learned to frame a comment in a way that starts a conversation. Saying something like, "I notice you've lost weight. What made you decide to do that?" allows the person to talk about their feelings about their weight rather than us interjecting our feelings (as sincere as they might be) about their weight first.

Just know, if you lose weight because you want to, I support you. But also know this: you look great, you are great, just the way you are right now. Don't let anyone (especially someone who's supposed to love you) tell you otherwise. Trust me. As an ex-member of the Pretty Face Club, I know what I'm talking about.

8. The Post-Divorce Years

"My life in two sentences: My husband and I have decided to separate. I'll be moving to Pittsburgh next week."

—Lynn's Weigh blog entry, October 25, 2010

When Larry and I ran into each other in a coffee shop in 1996, we hadn't seen each other in more than two years. When we hugged hello, it felt as if some force had willed us together.

We were married in 1998.

Looking back, we both see how our life together was framed by my children and his. Parenting and stepparenting were the foundations of our relationship. When the children no longer lived with us or needed us full time, our relationship seemed to outgrow its usefulness. By 2010, we were moving in different directions and we ran out of things to say.

For months, I felt as though we'd let people down: our friends, our family, and, for me, my readers. But Larry's and my relationship was not communal, and our separation had little if any impact on anyone, including our children. They and others sensed, but did not say, that for several months Larry and I had reached the end.

I was forty-seven years old, and other than the three months I lived by myself after I graduated from high school, I had never lived alone. I didn't expect there to be a learning curve for living single, but when I moved away from Larry and the town I'd lived in for years, I quickly realized I truly didn't know how to live separate from anyone.

Hot Water's On the Right
Posted November 2010

"Mom, there's no hot water up here!"

Daughter Cassie was scrubbing the tub in the bathroom upstairs in my new place, a two-story dark brown duplex built sometime before 1900, which is probably how old the roof was, too. There was hot water in the kitchen, so we were perplexed. "We" was daughter Carlene, pseudo-son Ian, the Two Men and a Truck guys, and my soon-to-be-ex-husband.

"Never mind!" she yelled down a minute later. "The hot water's on the right!"

I feel like I'm living in Seinfeld's Bizarro World. The hot water's on the right, the refrigerator door opens on the left, and the stove is electric. I share a wall with neighbors and I have an attached garage. The living room walls are beige and the bathroom is carpeted. I have cable. I had none of these things a week ago.

I am living alone for the first time in twenty-nine years. And no matter how determined I am to learn how to live alone, I am homesick. I miss my house. I miss the relationship I used to love. I miss my gas stove and bare floors and the wainscoting on the walls. I miss my dog.

I am aware of the rumors circulating in my former hometown. A few people on the outside of my inner circle don't understand these recent changes. They presume to know, although they've not asked me. I choose to ignore them because the only person who knows my truth is me. As painful as it is, I will face it and live it, and I'll do it without the added stress of caring what other people think.

I suspect I will feel like this for a while. Maybe a long while. I fully expect that I'll drink warm water and wash my face with cold until I get used to the hot water on the right, this new home, this new normal.

Life Lessons in a Laundromat
Posted November 2010

The last box is unpacked. Pictures, prints, and mirrors are hung on the walls. The furniture is where I want it. The bathroom is organized. The kitchen is user friendly.

Now it's time to live here, settle into a routine, and find a mechanic, a gym, the library, the nearest liquor store, the post office, and a laundromat.

I used to have a washer and dryer in my basement. A nice convenience, of course, but going to the laundromat should be a no-brainer, right? You wash, you dry, you read a book to pass the time. On Saturday, I separated the laundry at home: a bag of whites, a bag of darks, and a bag of towels. I packed a book, my glasses, and my phone. I went to the bank and got ten dollars in quarters. I drove to the laundromat, unloaded my bags, locked the car, walked inside, set the laundry on the floor, and realized I'd left my soap and dryer sheets at home.

"Don't panic," I told myself, and I spied a soap vending machine on the wall. I put in a quarter and the quarter came out the coin return. I put in a different quarter and that quarter came out the coin return.

"It don't work," said a man leaning over the counter. "The change machine don't work either."

Damn it.

"Do you mind Gain?" asked a woman who was texting on her cell phone. "Cuz you can use some of my Gain if you want."

"Really?" I said. "Thank you."

She handed me her bottle of detergent and said, "I don't have any fabric softener, though."

"That's OK, I'll go over to the store across the parking lot. Community is a grocery store, right?" I asked.

"Yeah," she said, "but go to Family Dollar or Big Lots. It'll be cheaper."

I held out a handful of quarters to pay her for the soap, but she just smiled and said no, and pointed out which washers worked best before she resumed her text conversation.

After starting my wash, I went to Family Dollar for dryer sheets and back to the bank for more quarters. I had no idea it cost nine dollars just to wash three loads.

When I returned to the laundromat, my clothes were washed and I threw them in a metal basket on wheels. A man wearing sunglasses said, "Those two are the best," pointing at two large dryers on opposite ends of a row of six. I divided my wet laundry, put it in the two dryers, and took a seat on the sorting table.

I watched the Gain-sharing lady fold her clothes and place them in laundry bags. I rolled my eyes and mentally slapped my forehead. I had put my laundry bags back in my car after starting the washers, not thinking that my laundry wasn't going to walk out with me when it was dry. I hopped off the table and went back to my car to get the bags.

I returned to the laundromat the next day to wash bedding. I remembered to bring what I'd forgotten before. I loaded the sheets into one of the "good" washers and sat down in a white plastic seat to read my book. A man walked in with a laundry bag and a ten-dollar bill. He inserted the bill into the change machine only to have it spit back out.

"It doesn't work," I said. "But there's a bank down the street that will exchange that for quarters. Oh, and that washer right there? Yeah, it's one of the best."

Learning the Ropes
Posted April 2011

This week was filled with those first warm spring days, the kind that make you smile every time you breathe.

When I moved in to the front facing unit of a one-hundred-year-old duplex in November, nature was dormant and so was I.

Six months later, buds are bursting, birds are nesting, flowers are blooming, and my Seasonal Affective Disorder has migrated for another year.

I love spring in all its complexity, even this year. Gardening is an old friend, and it has been especially comforting as I stumble my way through this unfamiliar new life. Along with patient friends and a supportive family, one thing that sustained me through the unusually harsh winter were thoughts of my new yard and what was beneath its snow and leaves and decay of last year's growth.

This week we finally got acquainted, my yard and me, when I raked up, dug up, and pruned five thirty-gallon bags worth of compostable material and surveyed the early spring perennials and the beds in which they have emerged. I also planned what annuals I will plant in May and how much mulch I'll need.

While gardening is familiar, lawn work is not. I earned my allowance and spending money cutting grass as a kid, but I haven't pushed a mower in more than thirty years, let alone start one. The people who lived in the other unit, the ones who shoveled the walks this winter and would mow the yard this year, bought a house and moved out a few weeks ago, leaving yours truly with the keys to the shed.

Since the grass wasn't going to cut itself, I heaved the mower out from its winter storage and I looked for some kind of button thingy that I remember pushing to prime the engine for easier starting. Apparently that button thingy went out with the dinosaur. Mowers have advanced in post-ice-age technology.

I held up the metal bar on the handle and pulled (and pulled and pulled) the rope to start it, but the motor was having none of it.

"Hey, neighbor, want some help starting that thing?" a voice called from over the fence.

"How loud was I grunting?" I muttered.

I swallowed my pride and called back over the fence, "Yes, I could use some help."

Mr. Neighbor came over, and within a minute, he had the mower running. Like a patient father, he showed me how to move the throttle on the handle to start the mower properly. He insisted I try it myself a few times, and while that felt a little weird (I'm forty-seven for god's sake!), I adjusted the handle throttle and pulled the rope and, by golly, it started every time! On the outside I was totally cool, but secretly inside I was doing a *huge* happy dance.

By the time my lesson was over, it was too late to mow, so I dragged the mower to the porch and decided to mow the next day when Claire and Luca were there.

"This is Grammy's mower!" I said, pushing the red monstrosity out to the yard. "You two stand back while I start it, OK?"

Moments later...

"What's wrong, Grammy?" asked Claire. "Why won't it start?"

Pull. Pull. PUUUUULLLL! Damn it!

I looked at them. They looked at me.

"Grammy, why can't you start it?" Claire asked.

Sigh.

What I'd normally have done is swear a lot and kick the tires and blame the machine. But I had a three- and two-year-old depending on me to be a responsible grandmother, so I took a deep breath and went over in my head yesterday's instructions: "Pull the throttle up to start and, holding this bar, move it down to get maximum power."

I pulled the throttle forward, pulled the rope and yay! Mower power ensued!

Luca was impressed. He followed me all over the yard. Claire was more interested in using my hand tools to dig up rocks in the driveway.

As I mowed, I learned the lay of my yard. There are water-logged dips in the middle and water-deprived inclines on the sides. Whoever lived here before had a dog because there are round spots of dead grass. When I finished, I was sweaty and very happy.

I've gone outside more than a few times today and have peeked through the blinds to admire my work. I think my yard and I are going to get along fine. There's a long summer ahead, full of gardening and mowing opportunities. I look forward to that planned peace.

Life, as my sister-in-law always reminds me, is good, and it really is. Rough and bumpy as my lawn? Yes. Uncertain as spring? Yes. But we're doing it and living it every day, so why not progress in those day-by-day infinitesimal moments by deciding to learn how to, for lack of a better metaphor, prime the mower the right way and start it?

Let the Mauling Begin
Posted May 2011

Running away is laborious, and yet it burns no calories. That's sad considering I've done more running away than exercise the last eight months.

As a blogger of personal things, it's sometimes difficult to know what to keep and what to give away. Today I offer, as personally as

I can, the following as a way of explaining my infrequent postings. I framed it within the lyrics of the song "We All Need Saving" by Jon McLaughlin.

Thanks for sticking with me.

"Come on, come on. You have got to move on. This is not the you I know."

Last week found current me, the person I don't know very well, sitting on the deck of my former house with my former dog, gazing at my former gardens. I was crying. I miss my former life.

"This isn't real. It's just all you can feel. And that's the way that feelings go."

A friend told me that until I learn to live within the space of my new life with the same strength and determination with which I lost weight, I would be forever grasping for and holding on to bogus and temporary securities.

That pissed me off.

"I haven't lived alone in thirty years!" I argued. "I'm doing the best I can. What more is there to it?"

"You have to let it maul you," he said.

"Well I'm sorry Mr. I've-Been-Alone-for-Four-Years, but I don't want to be mauled by loneliness," I retorted. "It hurts and it's scary."

"Exactly," he sighed. "But in time, the mauling becomes a scratching, and that scratching a gentle touch, and it won't hurt as much and you'll be stronger."

After the second round of tears, I stood up, went to the garage for a pot and shovel, walked to the end of the garden, and dug up part of the chives I'd planted five years ago. I put the pot in the Jeep, gathered my things, said goodbye to the dog, and started driving home.

"When the cloud in the sky starts to pour and your life is just a storm you're braving, don't tell yourself you can't lean on someone else, cause we all need saving sometimes."

I cried for twenty miles before I called my friend.

"This sucks!"

"Yup. But you're not alone. And you will be OK."

"I don't know why it has to be this way and I don't know the cure. But please believe someone has felt this before."

I'm that someone who has felt this before, in 1983. I tried to be OK after my husband died, tried to live a new life. Following the funeral, as friends and family returned to their homes, I had to prepare to move out of mine. The farm was my in-law's business, and without Bruce, I didn't belong there.

One week after the funeral, I sold our livestock and grain.

Two weeks after the funeral, I gave away Bruce's clothes.

Three weeks after the funeral, I moved in with my parents.

Four weeks after the funeral, my breasts dried up like an old cow's, and I nursed our six-week-old daughter for the last time.

I spent the summer trying to get back the life I knew, to shed grief like a snake sheds its skin. But the more I searched for Bruce in every man's eyes and some peace in a bottle of eighty-proof something, the worse I felt.

My best friend was going to marry Bruce's best friend and both Bruce and I were going to be in the wedding party. After he died, I didn't want to be in the wedding anymore, and I went to their wedding as a guest. Sitting in the back pew in the same church I was married, watching the procession, I was crushed by jealousy and grief. Everyone was smiling, which I couldn't do, even though I truly was happy for my friends.

If I cried, I knew I would draw attention to myself and I'd be "Poor Lynn" all over again. Once everyone was up front and the service began, I did the only thing I knew to do. I left.

This time, this new life has to be different. I can't leave. And no man, no distraction, no amount of lying to myself is going to save me.

I write this not for sympathy, but rather to say that no matter what we lose—weight, love, gardens, money, friends—running away cheats us out of the mauling, which in time, I have to believe, becomes a scratch, and then a gentle touch, until finally, we find peace.

Like Buttons in a Biscuit Tin
Posted June 2011

Part 1

When I was three years, my mother bought a tin of biscuits for Christmas. It was turquoise blue with gold trim and white inlay, topped with a noble-looking knob. It looked European, but the tin was made in the U.S. and the biscuits were made in Hopkins, Minnesota. Still, it was the fanciest thing I'd ever seen.

Mom used the tin to store buttons that she snipped off discarded items of clothing, worn out shirts and coats mostly, and I used to sort through them on rainy or snowy days, examining each one like they were works of art, which some of them were.

I don't remember how I inherited the tin or when. It's been with me through several moves, including this last one, and I always display it in a prominent space. Over the years, I've added my own buttons and what I've noticed is that buttons now aren't nearly as pretty or intricate as they were in the mid-twentieth century. I can assure you we were not fancy dressers, and I'd love to know where Mom got the green shamrock button, but if the buttons in the tin are evidence, it seems more attention was paid to the decorative effect of buttons on clothes and coats back then. Buttons on normal clothes now look utilitarian; their only purpose is to hold things together, not make a statement.

Anyway, Claire recently discovered the tin, and since she's no longer putting anything and everything in her mouth, I opened it for her. Her eyes got as wide as the biggest jacket button in there, and she sorted through them the same way I did when I was little, by size, color and texture. Such a tactile pleasure.

Part 2

Last week I went hiking alone for the first time; a real hike at a place I'd never been before, Todd Nature Reserve. With a scant reading of its trails, I decided to hike Loop Trail, a two-mile hike that, according to the website, "winds through various forest habitats, including upland deciduous forest and the edges of hemlock ravines. The trail has rocky portions, one stream-crossing, occasional wet spots and moderate grades. Walking time: sixty minutes."

I've been hiking many times, but always with a companion, usually my ex-husband. I was a little nervous to hike alone, and it didn't help that: 1) when I got out of my car at the trailhead, there was a sign posted that read, in part, "If you encounter a bear..." and 2) I was also the only person there as the only other car was exiting the lot when I pulled in.

I walked toward and into a very Tolkienesque entrance to the woods, an arch of maple and oak trees. It wasn't long before I met up with the mud and the stream crossing, but each step was like adding a button to the biscuit tin. Some steps were ordinary and some felt like they were shaped like shamrocks. If I fell, too bad. I was the only one there to lift me up. If I slipped, I was the only one to catch me. If I was afraid, I was the only one who could comfort me. If I encountered a bear, well, someone would find me later.

Part 3

It's been eight months since I left the life I'd known for twenty years; not happily, but for the greater good of not only me, but my husband. After a few rough years, one of us had to flinch.

Leaving that comfort zone, which enveloped not only a marriage, but the town I called home, was the hardest thing I've ever purposely done. My initial instinct was, as always, to find substitute comforts, but I slowly learned that's not how life works. You don't replace what was familiar with things you've only test driven. I had to step back, reevaluate, and start listening to my heart and gut rather than my head, with its ceaseless thinking, planning, and convincing me it's always right.

One. Thing. At. A. Time.

Every one thing we do adds up, like adding buttons to a biscuit tin. Pretty soon you have an eclectic collection of experiences.

For instance, while I love the healthcare professionals who took care of me in my former life, for practical and financial reasons, I had to replace them with local folks. I have a new primary care physician, chiropractor, dentist, eye doctor, and physical therapist. I shop at a different grocery store, drink coffee from a different coffee shop, buy gas at a different Sheetz, buy wine at a different liquor store, bank at a different branch, and hike and bike different trails. I'm living the adage that the only way we grow is through change, and change demands we step outside our comfort zones.

How do we do that without losing perspective? By recognizing and not throwing away those anchors that tether us to who we are; those things that remind us what our lives are about. As I've moved and changed these last several months, I relied on my anchors more readily—those anchors being my children, grandchildren, friends, books, meditation, and silence. They have been with me willingly all the while. I just needed to remember I needed them.

Today I went hiking at Todd Nature Reserve with my friend Shari. I took her on the Loop Trail. She said, "I can't believe you did this by yourself."

Like buttons, I continue to add experiences, friends, and realizations that fortify my life. And when I have a bad day, I take out the memory of them and sort them, flip them over, look at their beauty, and appreciate them for the comfort they are.

The Polar Vortex
Posted February 2013

To survive, we need air, food, water, and shelter. Last week, on the two coldest days of the Polar Vortex so far, I had air, food, and shelter, but for thirty six hours, I was without running water due to what I thought was a burst pipe.

I had plans to be away for a few days, but would be home before it got seriously cold in order to open the cupboards under the sinks and place space heaters in front of them. In Minnesota, I never experienced a frozen or burst pipe, but a few years after moving to Pennsylvania, the pipes in my apartment froze, and I spent several hours in the basement thawing them with a hair dryer. This time, I had a plan. And you know how the universe loves a plan.

Confident that I was home in time for the deep freeze, I opened the door and walked into a lake in the kitchen as water hissed from a pipe under the sink. I stood there for a moment, confused, like the house yelled "Surprise!" Only there were no balloons, streamers or confetti, and there was definitely no cake.

When the shock wore off, I went downstairs and turned off the water main, and with every towel I owned, sopped up the flood in the kitchen. Next, I called my landlord, who called a plumber, who called me and said he might get a chance to stop by the next day. It was noon, the temperature was dropping, and I had one flush left in the toilet.

I needed water.

I have very little concept of distance or volume. I can't tell you how long my driveway is or how much gas it takes to fill the tank of my lawn mower. And if I guessed, you'd laugh. That's why I'm not an architect. At Target, I stared at the gallons of water on the shelf and wondered how much I'd need to get through a day, or at the very least, a night. I settled on ten and wheeled my purchases out to my car, cursing the minus ten-degree wind chill.

It was sobering to realize how much water I use to simply wash my hands, brush my teeth, and flush the toilet. Ten gallons seemed like so much, and yet by morning, there were only two left. With no plumber in sight, I headed back to the store to buy six more.

Cold, cold, ridiculous cold. My Jeep was not happy. My exposed skin was not happy. When I got home, I turned on the stove and mixed up a batch of whole wheat, low-fat chocolate chip cookies. I heated a gallon of water on the stove so I could wash dishes and poured another gallon in a plastic pan to rinse them, acutely aware that I normally use more than two gallons of water when I wash dishes in the regular way, when water magically comes out of the faucet.

My friend/more-than-friend Jim the Carpenter called and asked if the plumber had been there. No, I told him. I'll fix it, he said. I thanked him and told him I baked cookies. I didn't tell him they were whole wheat and low-fat.

Jim arrived with everything to fix a broken pipe—gater bites, a piece of copper pipe, and soldering equipment—because from what I told him (in my "The pipe is hissing!" voice), he thought the pipe was split. I followed him downstairs and stopped just before the entrance to the creepy dark room under the kitchen. I've never been in that room because the bulb is burned out and I've read a lot of Edgar Allan Poe. Jim scanned the wall with his flashlight and said all the pipes were fine.

We walked back upstairs and he looked under the sink. He found the valve to the outdoor water spigot (*so THAT'S where it is!*) and turned it off. He went back to the basement, turned on the water main, and, voila, no hiss, no leak.

The valve, he explained, had most likely froze due to the skimpy temperatures a few days before, but I was only half listening. The sound of the toilet tank filling was like a symphony.

Ready!
Posted April 2013

Alice will do anything for beef jerky. Anything, that is, except climb the thirteen steep and narrow stairs to the second floor of my ancient duplex. One friend said climbing them is akin to scaling a wall. Not an unfair comparison considering you have to ascend and descend sideways, gripping the handrail like a safety rope. It's no wonder four-legged Alice was intimidated.

For two-and-a-half weeks, I bribed Al with jerky. I would place a bit of it on the first step and she'd reach for it, no problem. Second and third steps were easy, too. The fourth step required a bit of stretching, but with some snout-and-tongue maneuvering, she got it.

The fifth step took some contemplating and pacing back and forth across the threshold. After she had time to think about it, Al would skittishly place her front legs on the first step and stretch just far enough to nab the jerky before running into the dining room to feast. When I set a jerky on the sixth step, she looked at me from below like, "Um, no, human. I don't want a treat that bad."

We practiced a few times every day, and every day she got to the jerky on the fifth step and left the one on the sixth, and every night she looked longingly up the stairs when I went to bed.

I was about to lose hope, when last Wednesday evening I heard something moving around upstairs. I looked around for Alice. She wasn't on the couch or in her crate or sniffing around the garbage can. The windows and doors were all securely shut, so she hadn't escaped. The only place she could be...

I looked up the stairs and there she was, peering at me from around the corner of the spare bedroom, her tail thumping against the door, like she'd discovered the secret passageway to Narnia. She ran down the stairs, licked my hand, and ran back up. She slept on her dog bed next to my bed all night, and she greeted me with a big dog kiss when I woke up. It was a great morning for both of us!

I don't know what motivated Alice to climb the stairs on her own, but I find inspiration in her actions. No amount of bribing, cajoling, firm tones, soft tones, or words of encouragement were going to convince her that climbing the stairs was in her best interest. Only she knew what was right for her and when.

Brave Alice and her determination to discover what was at the top of the stairs is no different than you or me or anyone else who finally says, "I'm ready!" to make a change we long for. Changes, big or small, have the best chance of taking hold when we proceed on our own terms and in our own time.

"Ready!" doesn't always mean "I'm super confident that I can succeed!" It just means we're willing and prepared, as best we can be, to take a chance on the process with the hope that the outcome will be in the ballpark of our expectation.

The Department of Happiness Has Reopened
Posted October 2013

I was all, "Look at me doing the advanced aquarobics class!" last week at the Y, jogging vigorously in the pool and plunging Styrofoam dumbbells into the water and making figure eights. I felt the burn in my calves and the burn in my biceps, and then I felt…slippage, as in, the bottom of my bathing suit was slowly creeping down my bum. I dropped the dumbbells and probably looked like I peed as I tried nonchalantly to pull up my bottoms, but the instructor noticed the barbells floating around me and mouthed, "Wardrobe malfunction?" My face turned a million shades of red, and the class, reading her lips, broke out in laughter.

Apparently the string on the bottoms is essential. Who knew?

The string had come out in the wash and everyone knows what a pain in the butt it is to thread those things back through. But what doesn't seem essential at the time has a way of making its lack of use known, sometimes with embarrassing consequences.

There's been much talk since the government shutdown about what and who is "essential." It's got me thinking, especially since my bathing suit debacle, about the personal essentials in my life: eating right, exercising, relationships, love, *Call The Midwife*, *Downton Abbey*, and the Pittsburgh Pirates. But food, the gym, and Netflix aside, I wondered what essentials I've "laid off."

Earlier this year, I outlined my intentions for 2013, and one of them was to remember that I am responsible for my own happiness. This was inspired by Buddhist teacher and psychologist Tara Brach, who in a dharma talk asked people to reflect on these questions: "Do you experience happiness much? And when you're feeling happiness or well-being, are you aware of it? Is it something you're mindful of? And do you have a sense of what gives rise to happiness when it happens? What is it between you and really being happy, being contented?"

The core teaching of the Buddha is that what we want most is to change the source of suffering, that we want what is to be different, whether it's ourselves, our circumstances, our health, our parents, our lover, traffic, the price of gas. We think forward and forget now. We plan and we want. And there's a place for those things! Goodness, without want and desire, we'd never get anywhere! But it's where we place those things in our lives that matter. It's in how we think about what we want to be different and how we crave things to be different.

Lately, in wanting too many things to be different, I've slipped back into thinking that happiness is something that simply happens out of nowhere, even though I know that happiness is a choice. No one and nothing is responsible for making me happy.

This is the Chinese Year of the Snake. For a while now, it was mine as well. I've slithered through a lot of issues, circled a lot of decisions, and hissed at the changes I've had to make. I was happy only when happy presented itself. Now, instead of waiting for it to grace me with its presence, I am aware, once again, that happiness is a verb. It's something I do, not something I wait for someone else to do for me.

Happiness is as essential as the string that holds up my swim suit bottoms, and doing happy, at times, can be as complicated and aggravating as rethreading the string. Still, I choose presence. I choose awareness. I choose happy.

Letting Go
Posted December 2013

Since Christmas, I've been looking at 2013 through a mental wide-angle lens, reading my blogs and perusing photos, searching for a theme that sums up my year. Nothing really popped out at first. I met Jim in January, grandbaby Audrey in February, and Alice T. Dog in March. Carlene is Carlene. Cassie is Cassie. Kevin became a mechanic and moved to Asheville. Andrew is still in film school and my ex-husband retired from teaching school.

When I zoom in on the year a little closer, I can see that, by golly, I slowly got my brave on. Well, perhaps "brave" is a bit brave, but compared to last year at this time, I feel a little like Hercules! Despite repeated mistakes, indecision, giant emotional potholes on the path, and what felt like a physical apocalypse, 2013 offered me a lot of focus and awareness.

A quote that sums up this year is from Anne Lamott's book, *Help Thanks Wow*: "When you get your hooks out of something, it can roll away, down its own hill, away from you. It can breathe again. It got away from you, and your tight, sweaty grip, and your stagnant dog breath, the torture of watching you do somersaults and listening to you whine, 'What if?' and 'Wait, wait, I have ONE more idea…'"

Hoping something or someone will change is like getting mad at turbulence, something I actually did on a flight to Minnesota in November. It's futile. A waste of time. And yet, for so long, with my stagnant dog breath, I had my hooks in things I wanted so badly to be what I wanted them to be and refused to see what they really were. People, my knees, turbulence, that slice of cheesecake—I wanted them to be different.

I wanted *me* to be different.

Taking my hooks out of some (not all, by any means) of those things and people that weren't what and who I needed them to be, I was able to see that they were just being what and who they were designed or needed to be. In letting go, I set myself—and to some degree, them—free.

It wasn't easy. Sometimes letting go is like shaking tape off our fingers or picking a fleck of shell out of an egg in a frying pan. But those little leaps of faith didn't tear my world apart. They made my world less cluttered.

I'm heading into 2014 with a bit more courage and clarity than last year, but sans a Hercules costume. Perhaps granddaughter Claire will let me borrow her ninja mask.

Lynn Haraldson

When Love Comes to Town
Posted January 2014

I start a lot of pieces of writing on scraps of paper that I sometimes transfer to a Word document. I save the file as whatever the first typed words are, so the file name rarely makes sense when I see it days or months later. Every once in a while, I go through that no-man's land of strange file names to see if any of them are still relevant. Most of the time I have no idea what inspired me to write a particular sentence or short paragraph, so I exile those files to the electronic version of the Island of Misfit Toys.

During a recent file purge, I opened one I'd saved shortly after passing my motorcycle permit test in April. I called it, "I believe." I remember writing that I believed I could learn how to operate a motorcycle, but the last sentence completely slipped my mind: "I believe I can love someone."

Before sending the file to the Folder of Misfit Docs, I thought about April and where my thoughts were at that time. One of my personal goals in 2013 was to get to the heart of my commitment issues and my fear of letting go and moving on. For the most part, 2013 was a good year of letting go of what needed to go and letting in that which was best to be let in. This laid the groundwork for the leap of faith I took last week when I moved to a small town sixty miles east of Pittsburgh. I moved because I believe I can love someone, but not in the way it might appear on the surface.

I don't know if this is true for everyone who is single and in a new love relationship at age fifty, but I find it vastly different than being single and in love at age twenty. My life no longer centers around wanting or raising children. I have the luxury of being selfish with my time. I like sleeping in the middle of the bed. I enjoy the silence of living alone, and I can take out my own garbage. Loving someone at fifty is something I *want* to do, not something I think I need or have to do, which was what love felt like at twenty, thirty, and even forty.

When I say I believe I can love someone, I mean, specifically, that I believe I can love Jim *and allow him to love me*, idiosyncrasies and all.

Viewing ourselves through someone else's eyes is a portal through which many of us would rather not look. I mean, we're accustomed to who we are day by day, moment by moment. Who we are is who we are. Even if it is our desire to change a particular behavior, we still have a general understanding of who we are. Filtered through someone else's lens, our thoughts, actions, and physical appearance is interpreted in a way we cannot control or, for the most part, influence.

At age twenty, our life experiences stack up like helium balloons. At age fifty, they look more like phyllo dough. At fifty, we've spent more time in our bodies, taken in and dispersed vast numbers of opinions and advice, and have pretty much decided what's what. Some of us tweak our points of view and are open to new ideas, but mostly we're like, in the words of Edie Brickell, "What I am is what I am…"

And what I am in this new house and in this new town is a woman whose demons and joys and life lessons moved here along with dishes and furniture and photos of grandbabies. I'm here because I want to love and be loved, to work in my field, to ride new bike trails, drink coffee in a new coffee shop, and add more layers to that phyllo dough of experiences. (Anyone else hungry for baklava?)

I'm more willing to see myself through someone else's eyes and to filter that through my own understanding of who I believe myself to be, physically and psychologically. That makes it even more fitting that I moved to the hometown of Jimmy Stewart. His boyhood home is up the street from where I live. I've not always seen it or felt it, but mine is, and always has been, a wonderful life.

Lynn Haraldson

Care in the Time of Covid-19
Posted May 2020

In a recent poll, fifty percent of Americans said that the pandemic has negatively affected their mental health. My guess is the percentage is much higher because, you know, denial. "I'm fine!" is our trained response to "How are you?" even when, or perhaps especially when, we ask ourselves.

I've been thinking about what it means to care about people in the abstract and people we know up-close and personal, including ourselves, and how we can't effectively have one without the other. When I saw a recent photo of a large, white (and unmasked) man screaming in the face of a state trooper in Michigan during a protest against government mandates put in place to flatten the curve, my initial thought was, 'Wow, what a jerk!' and then, after some time to think, I wondered, What do we have in common?

Take away his disregard for the health and safety of those around him, I saw a person whose actions were motivated by fear (both rational and irrational) and not by an overarching compassion for humanity. The phrase "The government can't tell me what to do!" is not born out of anger. Anger itself originates in fear, and in this case, fear that the government can, and will, tell people what they can do.

There will always be folks who lose their shit and those who keep it together no matter what crisis they're faced with. While I am often the former, I live with the latter, one such folk who keeps it together. Even though Jim feels the underlying emotional impact of the uncertainty right now, and the fear of "What if I get it?" and the economic toll it's having all around, he expresses his fear by caring about people, not screaming in their face.

Here's what I mean. You know when you've reached the end of your rope and you can't type another word or read another word or watch another minute of news? I reached that place on Friday. I couldn't think anymore. I needed to talk to Jim. I slipped on my shoes, grabbed my cane, and started walking across the yard to the garage, gathering emotional steam along the way.

The dog had run out of the door ahead of me and she announced my arrival. Jim appeared in the doorway and his smile quickly turned to concern.

"What's wrong?" he asked, and all that pent-up fear disguised as anger came tumbling out.

"I miss my kids, I miss my grandkids, my knee hurts, and I'm a horrible writer!"

He wrapped his arms around me and I sobbed into his sweatshirt for what felt like an hour. When I started to pull away, he pulled me closer, and I cried even harder.

"You did the right thing coming out here." He knows I would stew in silence, or make mountains out of mole hills that had nothing to do with what was really bothering me, kind of like the protester.

We sat down and devised a plan for a social distancing visit with my daughters and the grandkids the next day. There was nothing we could do about my knee except talk about it, but acknowledging that it's messed up and needs to be replaced helped untangle the abstract fear I have of never walking again. As for being a horrible writer, I know this is not true, but the fear in that statement is that I'm not good enough and that I'll never be good enough, and saying it out loud lay bare that fear, too.

Jim didn't, and he can't, take my fears away. Only I can do that. But saying them out loud took them down to their bones and they became more manageable.

Lynn Haraldson

Epilogue

In nine years, through the loneliness and self-doubt, the fear and the clinging to things and people I had no business clinging to, I have learned to be my best friend.

Jim and I are still together, despite of and because of the heartaches and physical issues that have beset our relationship. It's a lot of work, as is any committed relationship, and we're not always good at it. But love gives us the dogged determination to hang in there.

I want to be in our relationship. I don't have to. That has made all the difference.

As for Larry, he is remarried, and our children remain the heart of our relationship. We run into each other at our grandchildren's birthday parties, and we still co-parent by occasionally butting our noses into our children's lives.

Lynn Haraldson is a blogger and award-winning columnist who has been featured in *People* and on *Oprah*, *Today*, CNN, and *60-Minutes Australia*. For more than twenty years, her writing has resonated with readers through universal themes of loss, body image, parenting, and, more recently, aging. She lives in rural western Pennsylvania with her little dog, Zuzu.

Visit her website at www.zenbaglady.com.

www.ingramcontent.com/pod-product-compliance
Lightning Source LLC
Chambersburg PA
CBHW030319100526
44592CB00010B/495